Your **Outta Control** Puppy

Teoti Anderson

T.F.H. Publications, Inc.
One TFH Plaza
Third and Union Avenues
Neptune City, NJ 07753

This book has been published with the intent to provide accurate and authoritative information in regard to the subject matter within. While every precaution has been taken in preparation of this book, the author and publisher expressly disclaim responsibility for any errors, omissions, or adverse effects arising from the use or application of the information contained herein. The techniques and suggestions are used at the reader's discretion and are not to be considered a substitute for veterinary care. If you suspect a medical problem, consult your veterinarian.

ISBN 0-7938-2900-3

www.tfhpublications.com

Contents

How Did
My Puppy
Turn Into a Monster?

In This Chapter You'll Learn:

✳ How to formulate a plan to deal with your outta control puppy

✳ What are normal puppy behaviors

✳ Common myths about "bad" behaviors

You fell for it, didn't you? Those soulful, dark eyes and that wagging tail. Couldn't you just see a halo sparkling over that adorable puppy's head? You knew you were meant to share your lives together in peace, harmony, and lifelong friendship.

What happened? When did that sweet puppy turn into a raving, outta control monster? Was it something you did? Something you didn't do? And more importantly, is it too late to fix? Can you get some control before the monster destroys your house, alienates your family and friends, and drives you nuts? You need first aid for your relationship—stat!

In order to live harmoniously in your household, your puppy needs a leader that can provide guidance and training.

You've got it. This book will help you pinpoint the problems that you're having with your puppy and provide effective, easy-to-understand solutions to help you gain control of the situation. Because right now you may be more worried about how to survive living with this outta control creature. Instead of covering typical basic training exercises, like "sit" or "down," this book is a first-aid kit for problem behaviors.

We'll give you a game plan you can follow to tackle the most common outta control puppy problems. In the meantime, we encourage you to start a reward-based training program that covers the basics and enhances what you learn here. If you happen to have more serious issues with your puppy, like aggression or fearfulness, we'll give you tips to get you started and explain how you can get more extensive help.

You'll learn how to take back your household and become a leader, without becoming a dictator. There's no need to use old-fashioned methods—those outdated "alpha rolls," scruff shakes, rolled-up newspapers—in order to tame your wild puppy beast. Using those methods can cause your puppy to mistrust you, and in many cases, can make your problems much worse. In addition, not everyone in your household may be able to do them effectively. Sure, you might be able to flip your 95-pound Mastiff puppy upside down, but could a toddler? Of course not! You want your dog to be able to work for the entire family, not just the person with the firmest hand. Instead, you'll learn to tame the wildest puppy with management, training, and tasty treats. You'll literally have that pup eating out of your hand! Most of all, it's *fun*. We'll teach you how to put the fun back into your relationship.

You can love your puppy without loving his outta control behavior.

After all, you still love that little monster, don't you? Despite your troubles, one sloppy puppy kiss and you still melt. That's great, because you can still love your puppy without loving some of the things he does.

Is Your Puppy Outta Control?

Does your puppy:

* Nip you all over, sinking his needle teeth into your skin?
* Jump on you a lot?
* Chew everything? Furniture, plants, your kids' toys, magazines, socks?
* Not listen to anything you say?
* Bark a lot?
* Hardly ever come when he's called?

How Did My Puppy Turn Into a Monster?

All puppies have innate, perfectly normal behaviors that can be difficult to live with.

✳ Growl when he plays tug of war?
✳ Act generally hyper, running all over the house like a speed demon?

If you answered yes to most of these questions, your puppy is normal. All of these behaviors are perfectly normal for the average puppy.

Many owners do not know what normal puppy behavior is like, so they get worried, thinking they must have accidentally brought home a mutant creature disguised as a cute puppy. Rest assured, your puppy is probably very normal—a monster, but he's a normal monster. All these behaviors are just what puppies do. This doesn't mean that we like all of these behaviors.

Here's another consolation for you—you are not alone. There are thousands of puppy owners just like you, yelling, "No! No! *No!*" all over the house, wondering what became of the fluffy angel they brought home. They're wrestling with the same behavior problems you are.

What's Normal for a Puppy?

As humans, it's easy for us to forget sometimes that puppies are not really little humans in furry suits. They are so smart and funny that we sometimes expect them to do things that are completely unrealistic for their species or age. Many people get frustrated when their puppies chew things up or have accidents in the house. These behaviors are annoying to humans but perfectly understandable in a baby dog. Puppies can't hold their bladders as long as adult dogs. They are teething, so they chew more. They are young, so they often have more energy than their adult counterparts. They have the attention span of turnips, and they don't

The More The Merrier?

Do you have more than one puppy at home? Perhaps you brought home littermates? Then you probably have twice as much chaos on your hands.

Many folks think bringing home littermates will be good company for their puppies. After all, dogs are pack animals, right? And at first, it looks like it's going to work. They play and play all day, wrestle with each other, do everything together. They're built-in puppysitters. Then it slowly starts to sink in that neither one of them listens to you. They pay more attention to each other than they do you.

This is because each puppy spends more time with another puppy than with humans. Oh sure, you play with them and love them, but, most of the time, they are interacting with each other. The bond between them can be greater than the bond they have with you, which can cause trouble later.

If you have more than one puppy at home, it's important you separate them and interact with them individually for a little bit each day. Dogs are pack animals, but you want to be the leader of your pack. Make sure you form a close bond with each individual puppy so that both of them will have a reason to pay attention to you.

How Did My Puppy Turn Into a Monster?

If you have more than one puppy, spend time and interact with each of them individually.

have a clue what you're saying when you speak to them. Sometimes they figure out words because they match certain actions over and over again, but puppies are not born understanding our language.

So what's normal for a puppy? Here's a general outline of what to expect in your puppy's development:

Birth to Two Weeks
Puppies are born blind and deaf. They can taste and feel. They can't control their own body temperatures very well, so they huddle for warmth. They can wiggle around and move, just not very far or very well.

Three to Four Weeks
Puppies' eyes and ears open, and their first teeth come in. They begin to wobble around, wag, bark, and explore their surroundings. The brain starts receiving messages.

Five to Seven Weeks

Puppies start learning how to act like dogs. They chase, bite, bark, and interact with their littermates. The mother dog may begin weaning puppies around the fourth week. She also teaches them discipline, and they begin to learn bite inhibition — not to bite down too hard on their littermates. This is a very important time in a puppy's development; they learn many social skills from their littermates that will help them deal with humans and other dogs later in life. If they are removed from their litters during this time, they may have trouble becoming good pets.

Eight to Sixteen Weeks

It's the honeymoon period! Puppies are usually in their new homes by now and they are making you believe they are perfect angels. They follow you around like little ducklings and hang on your every word and movement (makes you feel special, doesn't it?). You are the center of your puppy's universe. All is right in the world. What many people don't realize is that it's really the calm before the storm.

Your puppy is just a baby—you need to show him gently how to behave in your household.

Puppies follow people around at this stage because their senses haven't fully developed yet. They haven't yet noticed there is anything but you around to follow. However, they are growing rapidly. Soon they'll be able to see the pretty doily hanging off the coffee table and

A puppy under eight weeks of age is best left with his mother and littermates until he matures.

notice the squirrel on the other side of the street. All heck is about to break loose, but at this stage, we humans are usually blinded by that fluffy cuteness.

This is also a crucial time in your puppy's development. If your puppy is not introduced to many different humans, environments, and other dogs by the time he is four months old, then a golden opportunity is lost forever for socialization. He may find these things frightening later, which can lead to shyness or aggression.

A challenge to socialization is a fear period puppies go through between 8-11 weeks. Depending on the puppy, the fear period could last a couple days or weeks. Puppies suddenly are afraid of things that may not have frightened them before. Anything that scares them during a fright period could have an impact later.

Your Outta Control Puppy

At the end of this period, people sometimes get frustrated if their puppies are not housetrained. Puppies may sometimes seem to understand the concept, and then the next day piddle all over your carpet. This is because they are still infants. They are just learning bladder control — a patient, proper housetraining effort during this time will pay off later.

Four to Six Months

At this age, puppies begin exploring their surroundings with a vengeance. If you thought he was housetrained before, he could prove you wrong now. He may start challenging you and stop coming when you call him. He will put everything in his mouth because he is teething. He is losing his baby teeth; you may find them in his tug toys or on the floor, or he may even eat them before you can grab them. As his adult teeth come in, they make his gums hurt, so chewing makes his gums feel better.

Newborn puppies are completely dependent on their mothers and owners for the care that they need.

How Did My Puppy Turn Into a Monster?

Six to Twelve Months

Socialization with people is very important to produce a well-adjusted, friendly dog.

Now puppies start developing sexually. You may notice behaviors in your unneutered male puppy you never noticed before, such as humping, marking objects, roaming the neighborhood, etc. Your female puppy can have her first heat anywhere from 6 to 12 months of age. Around nine months of age, a puppy's back molars come in, so there may be another strong teething period. If a puppy did not get enough socialization or training in earlier stages, you might start noticing problem behaviors now, such as growling, fearfulness, etc.

Twelve to Twenty-Four Months

A puppy's breed and size will determine maturity. Small dogs are usually considered adults at about one year, while larger dogs take two full years to grow into adulthood—some giant breeds take even longer.

Myth-Guided Youth

Even if your puppy is outta control, it may not be what you think. Here are some common beliefs about puppies, along with some explanations for their behavior.

✳ *My puppy doesn't listen to me!*

Have you taught your puppy what words mean? For example, every time you put your puppy's food bowl down, you could say the word,

"Asparagus!" After a couple days of this, you could say the word, "Asparagus!" and your puppy would get very excited. This is because you've associated the puppy's food bowl with the word.

Does your family use different words to mean different things? Maybe you say, "Sit" to your puppy, but your spouse says, "Sit down!" Puppy owners also often fall into the trap of yelling their puppy's name over and over again to mean different things. "Fido!" is supposed to translate into "Leave the cat alone!" "Get out of the garbage!" "Come here!" and "Stop that!"—all depending on the circumstances. A puppy cannot learn what words mean if they are not used consistently.

✳ My puppy is stubborn!

When a puppy does something wrong, people love to blame it on a stubborn attitude, but this is not often the case. Sometimes the temptation to do something else is greater than a puppy's desire to

As he matures and tests his limits, your puppy may challenge you or stop coming when called. Before labeling him as stubborn, make sure you are communicating in a gentle, clear manner

How Did My Puppy Turn Into a Monster?

follow your wishes. For example, if you call your puppy to come to you outside but there's a nice patch of stinky grass nearby perfect for rolling in, your puppy may find it hard to resist. It's just like asking a kid to leave his toys and come do math homework. Sometimes a puppy is really just confused as to what you want, or there may be something else going on altogether.

For example, there once was a Bulldog puppy in a training class who refused to leave the building. She dug her paws in, lowered her head, and wouldn't budge. Her owner even pulled out treats to entice her, but it didn't work. You might think, "What a stubborn dog! Those Bulldogs are known for that!" The trainer knew differently. She took one look at the puppy's body language and realized the puppy was really terrified. It turns out that there were huge machines right outside the training center's door that had just turned on as the puppy started to leave. They

There are many myths as to why puppies misbehave, but most problems can be remedied with training, clear communication, and consistency.

Your Outta Control Puppy

made a lot of noise, and they frightened the puppy. She wasn't being stubborn, she was scared!

Why is understanding this important? Because how we treat puppies often depends on what we perceive their motivations to be. This puppy's owner got angry and frustrated when she thought her puppy was being defiant, but turned sweet as honey and melted on the spot when she learned her puppy was really afraid. Once she wasn't angry at her puppy anymore, the puppy got enough confidence to leave the building.

Puppies understand your voice tone and body language, which are important aspects of training.

How can you tell if your puppy is really being stubborn? Get some good books on dog body language and behavior to help you understand your puppy better. You may be surprised at what he's really telling you.

☀ *My puppy does bad things on purpose. He knows not to do them, but he does them anyway!*

Puppies do not live the lives of criminals, plotting all night in basements for ways to make your life miserable. Puppies live for *right now*. You know how your puppy is so excited to see you when you come home from work at the end of the day? Ever notice that your puppy is just as

How Did My Puppy Turn Into a Monster?

excited to see you when you come back from taking the garbage can to the curb?

Puppies live for instant gratification. If it feels good now, just do it! They don't think about the consequences that might come later. It takes maturity and training to help them learn to control themselves.

Will My Puppy Be a Monster for Life?

Just because your puppy is outta control now doesn't mean he has to be this way forever. You can work to change his behaviors. But before we look too far ahead, let's figure out how he got this way in the first place. Learning from your puppy's past will help you prevent problems in his future.

Where the Road to Perfect Puppyhood Took a Detour

In This Chapter You'll Learn:

* How your puppy's breed or mix of breeds affect his present behavior

* How your puppy's parents affect his health and temperament

* How to care for your puppy to help prevent behavior problems

Your puppy took lots of paths that led him to where he is now. If you understand how you got here, it will help you better understand where you're going, and it could help you avoid mistakes that could make matters worse.

The first couple months of a puppy's life are vital to his development and shape his future behavior, but the map for your puppy's course started even before he was born.

What were your puppy's parents like? What breeds were they? What

Your puppy's parents have a big influence on his health and temperament.

size? What temperaments did they have? Were they friendly? Were they aggressive? Were they hyper?

What about the breeder? Was she knowledgeable? Did she screen for genetic diseases? Did she plan this puppy's birth based on physical health and a great temperament? After your puppy was born, did she get it off to a good start, both physically and mentally?

Whether you purchased a purebred dog or rescued a stray, some person somewhere let two dogs come together to create your puppy's genetic blueprint, and you're living with the results.

The Breed Blueprint

What breed or combination of breeds is your puppy? Breed characteristics help shape your puppy's personality. Of course, every puppy is an individual. If your puppy's breed has a tendency to be reserved with strangers, that doesn't mean you can't end up with a social butterfly. If your puppy's breed is supposed to love swimming, you may have one who hates the water. Every puppy is different, but it helps to look at the breed background to see where years of genetic planning (or sometimes ill planning), have shaped the puppy you have today. You want to find out all the wonderful things about your puppy's breed—and the not-so-wonderful things, too. That way you'll have a better idea of what to expect, and you can better prepare for potential problems.

Where do you find this information?

✳ Ask your puppy's breeder.

✳ Go to the library or bookstore and look for books on your puppy's breed. Try and find information that lists the good *and* bad things

Although every puppy is an individual, his breed characteristics will help shape his personality.

Where the Road to Perfect Puppyhood Took a Detour

about your breed; some of these books just gush about all the good qualities and leave out the less-than-perfect tendencies.

✳ Ask a professional dog trainer about typical temperament and potential behavioral issues. Ask if she gets many of your type of breed in her classes and what problems their owners experience.

✳ Ask a person who does rescue for that breed. Rescue volunteers often see the best and the worst of their chosen breeds, and they can give you a wealth of information on typical temperaments and other issues.

✳ Search the Internet. Visit the American Kennel Club (AKC) website at www.akc.org, look under Breeds, and write your puppy's breed club secretary for information. It's usually available for free or a small fee.

Dogs in the Sporting Group, like this Chesapeake Bay Retriever, need lots of exercise to channel all their energy.

Your Outta Control Puppy

✳ Ask your veterinarian. The vet is also a great source to find out potential genetic diseases in your puppy's breed. Physical condition can play a huge role in your puppy's behavior.

The AKC has categorized breeds into several groups, all which have distinctive characteristics and inherent tendencies.

Sporting Group

Examples of sporting breeds include the Labrador Retriever, Golden Retriever, Irish Setter, Cocker Spaniel, and Weimaraner. A very popular group, these breeds were created to hunt, flush fowl, and retrieve. They are strong, very active dogs; sometimes more active than the average family can handle. They are family-oriented and need to be with and work for people. Retrievers, especially, put everything in their mouths and love to carry around things, and if it's not going to be a duck, it's going to be your shoes, towels, or remote control.

Hound Group

Examples of hounds include the Basset Hound, Beagle, Dachshund, Greyhound, and Rhodesian Ridgeback. Most hounds were designed for hunting. Some track a trail with their noses, like the Bloodhound; some use their keen sight to hunt their prey, like the Borzoi. Hounds usually have amazing stamina, as they are bred for following a trail for quite some distance. This group has the

Herding breeds, like the Border Collie, are very intelligent and will herd anything, even people.

Where the Road to Perfect Puppyhood Took a Detour

Terriers have persistent and feisty attitudes, as well as a lot of energy.

reputation for being stubborn, but often times they are just following their genetic code. If they're following a trail, they tune out everything else. Some have quite the voice—if you're not prepared for a hound's baying, it's quite an experience.

Working Group

Examples of working breeds include the Akita, Boxer, Doberman Pinscher, Great Dane, and Siberian Husky. These dogs were designed to perform jobs. They pulled sleds, guarded property, and performed water rescues. These tasks required strong, physically powerful animals. It's easy to fall in love with these small, cute puppies and not realize the size they will achieve when they are fully grown. Another active group, these breeds need a lot of exercise or they can become outta control in a household.

Herding Group

Examples of herding breeds include the Australian Shepherd, Border Collie, Collie, Shetland Sheepdog, and Welsh Corgi. These breeds were created to control the movement of other animals, such as sheep, cattle, ducks, etc. They are smart—sometimes too smart, because they can get bored quite easily and get into trouble. They are sensitive and work well with people. If you do not have any sheep on your property, they will happily herd humans, so these breeds often get into trouble for chasing children or nipping at people's heels.

Your Outta Control Puppy

Terrier Group

Examples of terriers include the Bull Terrier, Cairn Terrier, Miniature Schnauzer, Scottish Terrier, and West Highland White Terrier. Terriers were designed to hunt and kill pests, such as mice, rats, etc.—even going underground to attack animals in their dens. They are persistent and are known for their feisty attitudes, which get them into trouble sometimes. Terriers often do not get along well with other animals, including other dogs. Some of them are small, and their size can trick people into thinking they are low-maintenance, but these dogs have *lots* of energy and need active outlets.

Toy Group

Examples of toy breeds include the Chihuahua, Maltese, Papillon, Pomeranian, and Yorkshire Terrier. Toys were designed to be companion animals. They need to be around people, but don't let their small size fool you. Toys can be terrors if you let them rule the roost. Folks have a tendency to spoil this group as they are so precious, which can create some bratty behaviors. Some are also quite talkative, which can either make a great watchdog or drive you to buy a set of earplugs. They do not do well with young children, because children do not understand how to treat these small dogs with respect and careful handling. Often, the toy may feel he has to bite in order to protect himself.

Despite their size, toy dogs can be tiny terrors and need just as much training as larger breeds.

Non-Sporting Group

Examples of non-sporting breeds include the Bichon Frise, Boston Terrier, Bulldog, Chow Chow, Lhasa Apso, and Poodle. This is a diverse group, so it's hard to pinpoint general characteristics. Some, like the Chow, can be fiercely loyal to its family but aloof and wary with strangers. Some, like the Bichon Frise, are cheerful dogs that love to entertain. Because this group is a catch-all, look for individual breed information to better understand your puppy.

Mixed-Breed Dogs

This is not an AKC category, because that organization only registers purebred dogs. If you have a mixed-breed puppy, you have a

Try to find out as much as possible about the background of your mixed-breed puppy in order to get clues about his behavior.

Your Outta Control Puppy

combination of qualities on your hands. Get information on all the breeds in the mix; for example, if you have a puppy that is half Labrador and half handsome stranger, get information on the parts you know.

Think about your puppy's breed or combination when you look at his outta control behaviors. Do some of them now make sense? If you have a Siberian Husky puppy pulling you all over the neighborhood, you're just a sled to him. If you have a Golden Retriever puppy that grabs your shoes and carries them around, he's just doing what his genes are telling him to do. However, this doesn't mean you have to resign yourself to these behaviors, but it should help you better understand your puppy's motivation and give you more patience in dealing with some of the things he does. Getting mad at a puppy for doing something his genes are telling him to do won't solve anything.

Meet the Parents

Your puppy is a direct result of his parents and their parents before them. Your puppy inherited his physical characteristics from his parents—the color of his coat, his body shape, his size—but that's not all. He also inherited their temperaments and their personality characteristics.

If you start with a sweet dog that loves people, chances are his puppies will be sweet and loving, too. If you have a shy dog who is afraid of things, then chances are she will have shy puppies. If you have a hyper dog that is outta control, you'll probably have outta control puppies.

If you had a chance to meet the parents of your puppy, then you have a good idea about how your puppy will grow up. If you didn't get the chance to meet them, then you can only guess. Just know it plays a huge role in your puppy's physical and temperamental character. Some things you will be able to affect with training and a quality environment, but you can't untangle the genes your puppy inherited from his parents.

The First Weeks

From our puppy growth timeline, you know how important those first few weeks of a puppy's life can be. If a puppy does not have pleasant experiences with a wide variety of people, other dogs, and environments during the first few weeks of his life, then that opportunity is gone forever. You can make up for lost time, but it's much harder work.

Your Puppy's Social Calendar

Dr. Ian Dunbar, the noted veterinarian, animal behaviorist, author, and the founder of the Association of Pet Dog Trainers (APDT), says all puppies should meet 100 people before they reach four months of age. These experiences should be pleasant ones so that the puppy learns to trust people.

Introducing your puppy to lots of people, especially children, will help him become comfortable in any environment.

Eek! The Vet

You may love your veterinarian, but from a puppy's point of view, the vet's office can be a scary place. Your puppy is put up high on a cold, metal table, someone pokes and prods him, and then sticks him with sharp things. Your puppy also has better senses than you do; he smells disease and medicine and hears the whimpers of scared animals in the back room. But the veterinarian's office does not have to be such a spooky place. You can teach your puppy that the veterinarian is his best friend, next to you, of course!

Every time you take your puppy to the veterinarian, bring lots of really tasty treats and ask everyone in the office to feed him.

At home, get a non-skid bath rug and give your puppy treats when he stands or lays down on it. Feed him all his meals on the rug. Then take the bath rug to the veterinarian's office and put it on the metal table during your visit. Your puppy will feel safer with better traction, and he'll have his "security blanket" with him.

If you only take your puppy to the veterinarian's office for shots, then he may start associating the office with bad experiences. In between appointments, bring your puppy to the vet's, ask staff members to each give him a treat, then go home. Your puppy will learn the staff is friendly and doesn't always hurt him. Please don't ask them to make a huge fuss over your puppy, because they are busy helping other animals. However, it takes only a few seconds to give a treat, and most veterinarians and their staff are happy to help you socialize your puppy. After all, if your puppy loves it there, it's easier for the staff to work with him to keep him healthy.

For example, Fido is born, and his breeder only lets her immediate family interact with him. So he's met the breeder, her husband, and their two children. Fido goes off to his new family, who already has one dog,

Where the Road to Perfect Puppyhood Took a Detour

and he meets them, their relatives, and close friends—and that's it, except the vet, who poked him with needles. He's met about a dozen or so people, and one of them wasn't very nice to him, from Fido's perspective.

When Fido is six months old, his folks decide he needs to go to a training class. When he gets there, he freaks out. He barks, lunges, and pulls, and is so excited that they are horribly embarrassed. Why is he outta control? Because he's never seen this many different people and dogs before in one place in his life. They are aliens to him; maybe he's frightened, maybe he's overexcited. It will take some work to get Fido to where he's calm and comfortable, because this is a new planet to him.

Many behavior problems can be attributed to medical conditions. Make sure your puppy gets regular checkups and has a clean bill of health before you start training him.

What about health concerns? Puppies are not fully vaccinated until they are about 16 weeks old, and that's when our socialization window slams shut. Many people are afraid to take their puppy out for fear their puppy will catch a disease, especially parvovirus, which is highly contagious and deadly. It can be done, but this is where you need to strike a careful balance.

Puppies can catch parvo and some other diseases where there are feces from infected dogs. If your puppy has not had all his shots, never take him to a public place and let him walk on the ground—this means pet stores, public parks, and your neighborhood. If you cannot guarantee that the ground has only been walked on by vaccinated dogs, you are risking your puppy's health. If you must go to these places, *carry* your puppy—especially at the vet's office. Instead, visit your friends' houses who have safe, vaccinated dogs and invite everyone to your place to socialize your puppy. Ask them to bring friends, so your puppy can meet as many people as possible. It'll be great for your puppy's social life—and yours.

Allow different people to handle and pet your puppy. The more people, other pets, and places that your puppy experiences, the better socialized he will become.

If the 16-week window has already closed for your puppy, and you didn't realize he needed such a busy social calendar, you may be seeing the behavioral consequences. Please don't beat yourself up over this. You just didn't know how important early socialization was, and now you do, so you won't make the same mistake again.

Your Puppy's First Home

Did your puppy spend his first few weeks in someone's home, an outside kennel, a barn, or a cage? This will have an impact on how your puppy behaves in different environments. For example, if a puppy is raised outside, then inside noises might be frightening. You rarely hear the vacuum cleaner if you're living in an outside run.

Where the Road to Perfect Puppyhood Took a Detour

Puppies raised outside in kennels also often do not get the important variety of human interactions they need to bond with humans later. For example, if your puppy spent the first six weeks of his life in a kennel just around his mother and siblings, only seeing a person when it was feeding time, he will be more bonded to other dogs than people.

Maybe your puppy was bounced around from home to home before he landed in your loving arms. Dogs are very much creatures of routine. They like to get up at the same time, eat at the same time, and follow a schedule. It's reassuring to them. A puppy that has never known a stable environment could be stressed and shy. He's not sure what's going to happen next. Find out what kind of upbringing your puppy had before you took him home—it could go a long way toward explaining his behavior.

Feeding a quality dog food will help your puppy to be physically and mentally healthy.

Your Outta Control Puppy

Your Puppy's Menu

You've heard the expression, "You are what you eat." The same holds true for puppies. If you feed your puppy a quality food, it will help him be physically and mentally healthy.

Some puppies can stop eating puppy food and switch to adult dog food even before they reach physical maturity, because, with some puppies, all those calories are just too much for them. It's like feeding Frosted Chocolate Sugar Crunchies to young children all the time. If your puppy is bouncing off the walls, ask your veterinarian about switching to an adult dog food.

A growing trend among puppy owners is to feed a raw food and bones diet. Raw diet fans say their dogs' coats are shinier, they have less health problems, and their teeth sparkle. If you want to try a raw diet for your puppy, be sure to do your research to make sure your puppy will get all the nutrients he needs.

When you're examining your puppy's diet, don't forget the treats. You may be feeding your puppy a quality food but loading him up on sugary, fatty treats. Those calories have to go somewhere—either your puppy's waistline or as an outward behavior.

Your Puppy's Exercise Program

How much exercise does your dog actually get a day? Many

Daily walks can help put your puppy on a reliable schedule and can be good exercise for both you and your pet.

Where the Road to Perfect Puppyhood Took a Detour

dog owners don't realize how much exercise their puppies really need.

Look to your dog's breed or mix of breeds. Is there a sporting, herding, hound, or working breed in those genes? If so, your dog's genes are screaming at it to go, go, *go*. A leisurely walk around the block isn't going to cut it.

Dogs that are bred to retrieve, herd, hunt, or work, even if you don't use them for those purposes, still have the genetic program in them to do their original job. For example, Border Collies were made to run pastures all day, gathering sheep, moving sheep, and singling out sheep over miles and miles for shepherds. If you don't have any sheep for your puppy to work with, a quick jog around a suburban neighborhood is not the equivalent exercise.

If you provide your dog with regular exercise, he will have less energy to misbehave.

Your Outta Control Puppy

Got a retriever? Retrievers were bred to go out, get the dead bird, and bring it back, through fields and water and tangled brush, over and over again. A five-minute game of fetch is not the same thing.

If you have a really hyper outta control puppy, one that tears around your house, jumps on everyone and generally acts like a cyclone on speed, then there's a good chance he's not getting the true amount of exercise he needs.

Your puppy needs a lot of attention and activity. It is your job as his owner to provide him with a safe outlet for entertainment and play.

Letting your dog loose in a fenced yard by himself is not exercise. Most dogs run around for five minutes and then plop down and wait to be let in. A brisk walk around a block or two also is not enough. Depending on the type of dog you have, here are a few suggestions for sustained, cardiovascular puppy workouts.

* A 20- to 30-minute game of fetch.
* A brisk walk for several miles.
* Puppy playdates with other dogs.
* Putting your puppy's meals in a hollow toy, like a Rhino®, so he has to work to get it out.

You do need to be careful. If your puppy is under a year, or under two years for a giant breed puppy or mix, don't encourage him to engage in

Where the Road to Perfect Puppyhood Took a Detour

activities that cause impact on his tender, growing bones. This includes agility, flyball, or jogging. These activities are safer for dogs who have reached their full growth. When your puppy is old enough to take on these activities, you'll have to condition him just like any other athlete. After all, you didn't run a marathon the very first day you laced up your running shoes. Start slow and build up your puppy's stamina.

Also, if you live in a hot climate, make sure your puppy exercises during cooler times of the day so as not to overheat. If you have a question about the types of exercise that would be the most beneficial to your puppy, please consult your veterinarian.

A good dog is a tired dog. If you exercise your puppy's mind and body, he will have less energy to indulge in destructive behaviors.

The Role You Play in Your Puppy's Personality

In This Chapter You'll Learn:

❋ How to deal with your puppy's unacceptable behavior

❋ How to reward your puppy for good behavior

❋ How to be a good friend and role model for your puppy

We've looked at your puppy's background for clues as to why he ended up outta control, but now comes the intimidating part—looking in the mirror.

Some folks are eager to admit they probably made mistakes in raising their puppy, "I know it's my fault. I spoiled him when he was little and now he runs the house." But many people are embarrassed. Let's face it; none of us wants to admit we goofed. But if you figure out where you went wrong, you can fix the problem and get back on the right track. So let's not place blame—let's find solutions.

Who's Training Whom?

Every time you interact with your puppy, one of you is training the other one. The goal is for your puppy to be the student more often than you are. Some outta control puppies are masters at turning the tables.

For example, your six-month-old puppy starts pitifully whining at 2:00 am. You promptly get up and let her outside to do her business, and then you go back to bed. Are you training your puppy to eliminate outside or is your puppy training *you* to leap out of bed before the hint of dawn and let her outside? A healthy, six-month-old puppy can hold her bladder all night just fine. She's just training you to let her out when she wants to go out.

Take the adorable fluffball who stares at you imploringly when you eat your dinner in front of the TV. He's so precious, you can't resist giving him a taste of your pizza. The next night he's back, resting his little chin upon your knee, and it's so cute that you give him a slice of your pot roast. In no time at all, he's a full-grown dog, pawing at you whenever you sit down to eat. The cuteness has long worn off. Worse yet, he does it to your guests, too. Your puppy has trained you to feed him when he looks cute and paws at you.

Owners often inadvertently reward puppies for bad behavior. It is better to ignore your puppy when he does something you don't like and only acknowledge him when he behaves.

Is it a puppy's fault he's so good at training humans? Does he deliberately plot against you? Not at all. Puppies do what works, just like people. If you do something and it pays off for you, you repeat the behavior, too. If you show up for work and do your job, you get a paycheck. You keep doing your job in order to get the paycheck. Dogs are very good at figuring out how to get a paycheck from us.

The choice to pay or not lies with us—we get to choose what we teach our puppies. It's just sometimes people make the wrong choices.

Take the previous examples: What would have been better things to teach these puppies? In the first case, it would have been great to teach the puppy not to whine in the middle of the night. To do that, all the owner had to do was ignore the puppy. The puppy would have soon realized it wasn't getting her anywhere, and she would have stopped. In the second case, if the owner had not fed the puppy while watching TV, the puppy would have learned that looking cute didn't earn him any food.

Here are some other common challenges that started with paychecks for the wrong behavior.

* *When I call my puppy, he runs away from me. It's just a game to him.*

Have you ever told your puppy to come, then ended up chasing and trying to catch him? Chasing is a *great* game to a puppy. He feels like the center of the universe, often with the entire family running behind him, "cheering" him on. The problem is that when you say, "Puppy, come." and start chasing, you are actually teaching your puppy to run away from you when he hears the word "come." So, you're right; it is a game to your puppy, one you taught him to play. Oops!

* *My puppy chews up my shoes or my puppy tears holes in my new socks.*

Have you ever given your puppy an old shoe to play with or maybe an old sock, tied in a knot? You've taught your puppy that shoes and socks are great chew toys. A puppy does not know the difference between old items you were about to throw away and brand-new items you have in your closet. Oops!

A similar problem comes from the growing popularity of stuffed animals as toys for puppies. They make stuffed toys especially for puppies, but puppies can't possibly know the difference between the stuffed hedgehog you bought for him and your daughter's prized teddy bear. They're all toys from your puppy's perspective.

Who's Your Puppy's Best Friend?

You know the phrase, "Man's best friend"? Well, the person or animal who is your puppy's best friend has the greatest influence upon him. We'd all like to think our puppies worship the ground we walk on, but

As your puppy's best friend, you have a great deal of influence on his behavior.

that's usually our egos talking. The truth is that two things pave the way to a puppy's heart—food and time with pleasant experiences.

Who feeds your puppy? If your spouse feeds your puppy, you may find your puppy listens to your spouse more than he listens to you. This is because your spouse is the "Keeper of the Big Paycheck." Your puppy has associated a wonderful thing, his meals, with this one person.

The more time you spend with your puppy, the easier it will be to train him.

Who spends the most time having fun with your puppy? Is it a person or perhaps another dog? Dogs are pack animals, and they bond closely with members of their family, the ones they spend the most time with. It's not uncommon for adults to come through dog training classes and get incredibly frustrated because their puppies do not pay attention to them. Then we bring Junior in and the puppy does everything the child asks. In these cases, it's pretty evident that Junior plays with the puppy more than Dad. The puppy knows Junior better and is more bonded to him.

If your puppy spends most of his days, perhaps in the backyard, with a canine buddy, then your puppy could bond more closely with the other dog than with the human members of your family. This happens especially with puppies that are kept outside all the time, or who are

The Role You Play in Your Puppy's Personality

only allowed in a garage or inside room during foul weather. These puppies grow up apart from the "main pack," so they're not as bonded to it as a puppy raised inside and in the middle of a family. That doesn't make it impossible to train these puppies, you just have to build up your relationship.

The more time you spend with your puppy, the easier it will be to get his attention and train him.

Who's In Charge?

There has been a lot written and said about being the "alpha" in your household and making sure your puppy isn't "dominant" over you. Some owners are terrified if their puppies look them in the eyes because they think their puppies are challenging them. Some worry if their

Your puppy should look to you for guidance and direction. Praise and reward is always more effective than punishment.

Your puppy may be outta control, but you should never be. Always remain composed when training or disciplining your puppy.

puppies get up on the bed, eat before they do, or go out the door first. The truth is, a puppy can look you dead in the eye, eat first, dash out the door before you, and practically live on your bed and be the most docile lamb you'd ever want to meet. Another puppy could do those things and be a ferocious lion. It all depends on many of the factors we've already discussed.

What *is* important is that *you* are the leader of your canine pack. Your puppy should look to you for guidance and direction. It is not a dictatorship. Save your hands for petting your puppy, not punishing him. If you use your hands for discipline, your puppy may grow to fear them, and it's heartbreaking to see a puppy that cringes from an extended human hand. Physical discipline is also dangerous because it can teach puppies to become aggressive.

The Role You Play in Your Puppy's Personality

Let's say you bring home a sweet, loving puppy. He's not housetrained, so every time he makes a mess in the house, you roll up a piece of newspaper and swat him with it; not hard, just enough to get your point across. At first, it seems to work; he clearly does not like the newspaper, but he's still having accidents in the house. In fact, he's gotten more sneaky about it. He's now pooping behind your couch. One day, you grab the newspaper to tell him he's wrong, and he lifts his lip at you. You swat him a bit harder, because you certainly can't have a dog defying you like that. The next time you try it, he actually growls. What's going on? Did you mistakenly bring home a mean puppy?

What went wrong is the method. A young puppy is not housetrained because he's a baby. He just knows he has to eliminate, he doesn't understand it's not okay to do it on your carpet. When you use a rolled-up newspaper, your hands, or any other physical method to show him he's wrong, you're trying to make the point he shouldn't eliminate inside. But the puppy may not see it that way. He may think you're attacking him for doing something very natural. When he tries to tell you he's upset, he lifts his lip—that's dog communication. When you react more strongly, *he* reacts more strongly to try and get his point across, because you didn't understand him the first time. He's not trying to be dominant or bossy, or anything like that. He's trying to talk to you in the way of his species. However, the more harsh you get, the more aggressive he gets. The more you escalate your physical punishment, the more you're teaching him that's how you solve problems. It's a vicious circle, and one that can lead to a serious dog bite. The great thing is that you don't have to prove that you're stronger than your puppy— just smarter. You can get the same results—in this case, a housetrained puppy—without resorting to physical punishment.

Does this mean you can't ever discipline your puppy? Not at all. This also doesn't mean you should be a pushover—far from it. You just need to learn to control your dog with your voice, not your muscles.

Reward your puppy for the behaviors that you like, and you will find that they happen more often.

In fact, you may need to learn some tough love lessons. Just because your puppy wants something doesn't mean he should always get it. If you indulge him, he could end up being a pushy adult. Some puppies never learn to emotionally handle not getting what they want because their owners give them everything, all the time. These owners then find themselves slaves to very demanding dogs, all because they had kind hearts and couldn't say, "No."

You can say "no" to your puppy. He doesn't have to get everything he wants, when he wants it. It's up to you to set limits and stick by them, and you can do it without using physical punishment.

The Role You Play in Your Puppy's Personality

Think of yourself as the coach of your puppy pack, even if it's just a pack of one. A coach sets the rules, makes sure the players follow them, helps educate players that don't understand the game, and encourages his team to win. You can do all these things with your puppy.

A good coach looks for qualities in his players and cultivates them to help improve the overall team. It's easy to lose sight of this when living with an outta control puppy. Sometimes you're so frustrated dealing with bad behavior that it becomes all you see. That's a dangerous habit to fall into, because your puppy will never get any better if all you see is his faults.

Try being a good coach. Can you see all your puppy's wonderful qualities hiding behind his outta control behavior? Find the behaviors you like and reward your puppy for those behaviors, and they will occur more often. For example, is your puppy passed out in the living room after a long day, lying there quietly? Tell him he's a good puppy. If you reward him for lying there quietly, he'll be more likely to do it again.

You may find your good coaching pays off in other ways, too. If you train yourself to look for the good things in your puppy, you'll start seeing them everywhere; in your spouse, in your children, in your job. It's all about relationships and how we deal with them. We can either complain about all our burdens or work to fix our problems and celebrate our successes. Start coaching your puppy for winning results for the both of you.

46

The Roles of Family, Friends, and Foes

You may not be the only person or pet in your puppy's life. What kind of role do others play in your puppy's training and development? A big one! Every person and animal that interacts with your puppy helps shape his behavior.

It's important that everyone have the same rules you do and is consistent with your puppy. Otherwise, it can get pretty confusing from the puppy's perspective. Let's say you use the word "Sit" to get your puppy to sit and the word "Down" for your puppy to lie down on the floor. But when your spouse wants your puppy to sit, he says, "Sit down." To your puppy, what do "sit" and "down" now mean? How is he supposed to understand that sometimes "down" means one thing and sometimes it means something else? This is very confusing. Make sure your family and friends use the same words you do with your puppy to mean the same things.

They should also have the same rules you do. For example, if you don't want your puppy on the furniture, then the entire family should follow that rule. If you scold your puppy for getting on the couch, but your kids encourage him to jump up, that's not very fair, and it's terribly confusing for your puppy.

Another common example is jumping. Many people do not want their puppies to jump up on them and try to teach them to stay off. Then you have certain family members or friends who encourage your puppy to jump

You must be consistent with household rules; for example, if your puppy is not allowed on the furniture, then there should be no exceptions or you will just confuse him.

on them, saying, "Oh, I don't mind. I love your puppy!" That may be fine for them, but what about a frail person? It's a hard concept for a puppy to understand that he can jump up on Uncle Joe but not on Grandma.

Sometimes it's not a person, but a situation. Mom doesn't want the puppy jumping on her when she's in her Sunday church clothes, but doesn't mind the puppy jumping up when she's in casual clothes. Puppies are not fashion hounds. They don't understand that it's okay to jump on jeans but not pantyhose. Make sure everyone in your life plays by the same rules so your puppy will learn them faster. If they don't, it will take your puppy longer to figure out the complicated terms, and he may never learn them.

Untrainers

There are usually a few folks in your life who, no matter how many times you ask them, just won't follow the program. You may ask Uncle Joe to *please* stop letting your puppy jump on him, but he does it anyway. You may beg your friends *not* to feed your puppy from the table, but they slip him tidbits despite your request. You may threaten your kids to stop teasing the puppy so he doesn't get all riled up, but they work him into a frenzy anyway.

These folks are known as Untrainers. For all the work you put into training your puppy, they untrain him. For every step you take in communicating with your puppy and teaching him manners, they drag him three steps back. Why does your training suffer? Because puppies do what works and what pays off for them. If you ignore your puppy when he jumps up, he'll stop doing it because it doesn't pay. But then an Untrainer comes along and hugs and kisses him every time he jumps up, which is a great puppy paycheck. If your puppy gets paid sometimes and not other times, it's inconsistent. He can't figure out the rules

Everyone who interacts with your puppy must communicate what is expected of him. Clear, consistent signals will help him learn faster.

because the rules keep changing, and the paycheck is different every time he does the same action.

Many times your Untrainers are not deliberately trying to undermine you; they just don't understand how their actions affect your puppy's actions. But every time your puppy interacts with an Untrainer, especially during the early stages when you're trying to teach him basic manners, it just confuses your puppy. Don't feel bad; there's usually an Untrainer in every family.

So what are you to do? Do you let your puppy be confused? Do you let an Untrainer undo all your hard work? It's better if you don't. If you make sure your puppy gets clear, consistent signals, then he will learn faster. If you let him stay confused, he can't ever understand what you expect of him. You may have to practice some of your tough love on the Untrainers in your life.

If Uncle Joe can't stop himself from encouraging your puppy to jump up, put the puppy away when Uncle Joe visits so he doesn't learn that jumping is okay. If your friends insist on slipping your puppy food from the table, put the puppy away so he can't pick up that bad habit. If your kids keep teasing your puppy, causing him to get mouthy and hyper, explain they can't play with the puppy unless they follow your rules. This is not meant to be harsh to your family and friends. You just need to set boundaries and stick to them if you ever want your puppy to stop being outta control.

You may have to train your beloved Untrainers just as you do your puppy. If you explain they are just confusing your puppy and getting him into trouble, then maybe they'll stop. If they learn their actions mean they can't play with your puppy anymore, that might encourage them to follow your rules. And if you reward them for interacting with your puppy appropriately, it will encourage them to continue.

Your whole family needs to set boundaries and stick to them if you want your puppy to succeed with training.

The Roles of Family, Friends, and Foes

For example, if you tell Uncle Joe he's a hero for only petting your puppy when he sits, then Uncle Joe will be more likely to do it again. If you promise your friends you'll serve an extra-decadent dessert if they ignore your puppy during dinner, that's a great incentive to shed their Untrainer ways. Tell your kids you'll give them points for every time you see them doing something right with the puppy, and the points will add up to a special prize or privilege. You'll have them helping you train your puppy in no time.

Reward-based training is contagious; once you start with your puppy, you'll find there are ways to use it with your family and friends, too. The reason why it catches on so quickly is because it works.

Foes

If your puppy is introduced to lots of nice people and other dogs, that will help him grow up to be a well-rounded, stable family companion. By the same token, if your puppy has bad experiences with people or dogs, it could have a negative impact on his personality. Unfortunately, sometimes our puppies have bad experiences with unkind people or vicious dogs, and it can cause problems that are very hard to fix. If you don't know anything about your puppy's background, then it's impossible to guess what kind of experiences he had before, but you can do your best to control the experiences he has while in your care.

Make sure anyone who handles your puppy knows how to do so in a safe, gentle, friendly manner. If you don't like what's going on, stop it. For example, if someone is teasing your puppy, holding him incorrectly so he feels unsafe, or tormenting him, don't let them. Some strange folks think it's funny to tease a puppy into a frenzy, such as grabbing at his paws or ears, going after his chew toys until he's upset, etc. But their amusement is a puppy's nightmare. This just teaches your puppy that

Make sure everyone who handles or plays with your dog knows how to do so in a safe, gentle, friendly manner.

some people aren't very nice and shouldn't be trusted, and your puppy could start thinking that way about every stranger he meets. Then you end up with a fearful puppy that may think it's better to lash out first before someone goes after him.

Some folks are just not familiar with puppies and don't know how to act around them. They may try and pick him up by his front legs, or pat, pat, pat him on the top of the head to irritation. These folks need your guidance to make sure they interact properly so that they don't frighten your puppy and accidentally teach him that people are scary things to avoid.

Don't assume that just because someone is a dog professional that they will treat your puppy properly, either. Before joining a dog training class, visit to check out the trainer. Make sure their methods agree with yours. When choosing a groomer, ask to watch her in action and get references

The Roles of Family, Friends, and Foes

from other customers. References are also a good idea when researching pet sitters and dog walkers. Interview veterinarians just as you would a pediatrician for your children. You are looking for people who are professional, knowledgeable, continue their education to ensure they are up to date on the latest information, and will treat your puppy with kindness and compassion.

Be careful when your puppy is outside and unsupervised. Some find it very convenient to leave their puppies outside during the day in their fenced yards, but bad things can happen to dogs without their owners there to look after them. It's a sad, common story to hear of puppies stolen out of their own backyards. Thieves use the puppies for breeding, sell them for cash, and some even use them as bait for dogfighting rings.

Puppies can also be teased by neighbors or children. You don't want your puppy to hate kids, you want him to love them and be gentle with

All the people in your puppy's life, including pet sitters, trainers, and groomers, should treat your puppy with kindness and respect.

If your puppy only meets other agreeable and responsive dogs, he will always make friends easily.

them. But bad experiences with children can cause puppies to have real problems. If the schoolyard bully pokes sticks at your puppy through the fence or throws stones over the side and laughs every time your puppy barks and growls, he's teaching your puppy that children are nasty creatures. Your puppy may think that all children are like this one, and may develop a fear of children overall. The next thing you know, your favorite niece comes for a visit, and your puppy barks and lunges at her. Small dogs, especially, can be rather wary of children in the first place. If you add a cruel experience on top of that, you may end up with a dog that growls every time he sees a child.

Problems can also occur with other dogs. Let's say you're walking your puppy and a stray dog runs up to you, growling, and attacks. You get away and your puppy is not seriously hurt physically, but emotionally he could be traumatized (Heck, you are, too!). Your puppy may start to think all other dogs are a threat; after all, he was minding his own

The Roles of Family, Friends, and Foes

It is important that your puppy spends time with his littermates while young so he gets along with dogs later in life.

business when suddenly attacked. This can make your puppy fearful or aggressive toward other dogs.

Sometimes it's not always an aggressive dog, but an overexuberant or socially inept dog that could frighten your puppy. If you let your small, quiet puppy have a play date with a big, bouncy, pushy dog, it could scare the fur off him. Different personalities or size may affect how your puppy reacts to other dogs.

It is important that your puppy learn that other dogs are great so that he won't develop fear or aggression issues with them later in life. Make sure you find safe, friendly dogs for your puppy to play with. Who knows? While you're looking, you may make new friends yourself.

It's terrible that one or few experiences with a poorly behaved child, adult, or dog can paint over all the wonderful children, adults,

Loose Dog

Dogs running loose are a real problem in this country; unfortunately, owners do not always take responsibility for their dogs. Some folks insist their dogs need to run free, not facing the fact that it annoys their neighbors and is dangerous for their pet.

Part of being a responsible dog owner means containing your puppy safely. An old-fashioned fence is still the best solution. If you can't afford to fence your entire yard, even a smaller pen will do as long as your dog gets plenty of daily exercise in safe activities.

One type of fence gaining in popularity is the electronic fence containment system. Aside from the fact this system doesn't follow reward-based training (it's not very rewarding to get an electric shock), these fence systems have drawbacks that many owners don't realize. For example, they don't keep other dogs out. Stray or loose dogs can come into your yard and harass or hurt your dog. Also, they don't always keep your dog in. If the motivation is strong enough, a dog can leave your yard, and he may not want to come back, since he knows he'll get another shock once he crosses the line back home.

If the product malfunctions, the consequences can be serious. It can cause the collar to repeatedly shock your dog, even if he's not near the fence line, or if you forget to replace the batteries, your dog may learn he can just leave the yard. More seriously, your dog may start associating different things with the electrical shock. Some dogs think whatever they are looking at during the zap is what caused the shock. This can cause dogs to be fearful and aggressive toward neighbors, kids on bikes, strollers, etc.

Some neighborhoods don't allow old-fashioned fences, so this can be a difficult decision for puppy owners. Just be sure you do your research in your goal to create a safe place for your puppy.

and dogs in the world, but it can happen. Please work hard to make sure your puppy learns the better side of all species.

Children

The challenge in making sure your puppy has good experiences with children is that you're dealing with babies of two species. Children sometimes have a hard time remembering what you told them. They have energy to burn, and they sometimes don't realize their own strength—just like your puppy.

Puppies see children differently than they do adults. Children are smaller, so they don't have the commanding height and corresponding assertiveness that adults have. Toddlers move awkwardly, like little robots, not smoothly like most adults. Kids make random, loud, high-pitched noises. They grab things really hard. All these characteristics can alarm your puppy. The differences between human children and dog children can also cause some serious problems.

For example, a puppy is mouthing Junior's hand. Junior shrieks and pushes the puppy away. The puppy comes back harder, and Junior gets louder, flailing his hands in an attempt to get the puppy to stop pinching him with those needle teeth. The situation escalates and the puppy nips Junior, who starts screaming and runs for Mom.

When Junior flails and makes high-pitched noises, this only excites the puppy more. The puppy does not interpret the sounds and actions to mean, "Stop." He thinks it means, "Keep going." Think of how puppies play with each other; they tumble, growl, and roughhouse. Shrieking and flailing is also prey behavior. (Yes, Junior is acting like a wounded squirrel!) This doesn't serve to calm your puppy down but to crank him up higher and higher. The puppy is not being cruel or vicious, he's just responding to Junior's behavior the way a dog would.

The ways that children play can often mean problems for a puppy, too. Little girls want to dress the puppy up and squeeze him in tight hugs. They may only be expressing their love for the puppy, but that doesn't mean the puppy interprets these actions as affection. Little boys can be impish and tease the pup, poking at her just to see what she does. These actions can cause your puppy to mistrust children. She will tell them to leave her alone by curling her lip, growling, or snapping. If they don't understand her communication and keep tormenting her, then she could bite.

Children can make great playmates for puppies; however, make sure your child knows how to behave around dogs and always supervise them closely.

You need to teach the children in your puppy's life to be gentle and calm. Running will only invite your puppy to chase them. Flailing and shrieking could incite your puppy to mouth or nip. This is hard, especially with younger children. You tell them something and they follow your directions for about five minutes, and then forget. You must be vigilant and make sure your children follow your rules. If you don't, you could end up with a puppy that dislikes children and feels a need to bite them to defend himself, as well as an injured child.

Just as you teach children to behave around puppies, you also need to teach your puppy to behave properly around children. Puppies should not be

The Roles of Family, Friends, and Foes

Just as you teach your child how to behave around puppies, puppies need to learn how to behave around children.

allowed to jump on children, mouth them, or steal their toys. The exercises in this book will help you control these problems.

Kids and puppies can be the best of friends, but it takes work and careful supervision to make sure the relationship is a healthy, safe one. Puppies, as well as grown dogs, should never be left alone with a child. Even the most perfect of adult dogs has a mouth full of razor sharp teeth. There have been cases of sweet dogs, always loving with children, who still bit after something happened. All it takes is for a child to trip over an older dog's arthritic hip, reach for the wrong bone, or engulf a sleeping dog in a tight hug. It often happens fast, the damage is often severe, and the family is usually taken by surprise. Be safe. Dogs and humans are different animals and misunderstandings can happen, especially between the younger of our two species. Never leave your canine alone with children, and you won't have to live through the tragedy of a dog bite that could have been prevented.

Other Pets

If you have other pets in your life, they may not welcome the addition of an outta control puppy. Sometimes things settle down on their own.

Sometimes animals never really get along, and, occasionally, they seriously hurt each other. Here are some tips to help.

✳ Do not allow your puppy to pester other animals. He needs to learn manners. In many cases, an older dog will discipline your puppy when he's had enough shenanigans. But if you have an easygoing older dog whose nature is to just take the abuse, then you need to stop it before it gets out of hand. Your puppy, being a youngster, may not know when to quit bugging his older playmate.

✳ Don't allow older dogs to terrorize young puppies, either. Some older dogs, especially adolescents around one to three years of age, may be too exuberant for your younger puppy and might accidentally teach him that other dogs are scary beasts. Please be careful, especially if there is a significant size difference. Smaller breeds are more fragile, and they can be easily hurt. For example, a rambunctious two-year-old Labrador puppy could squash a four-month-old Pomeranian puppy without meaning to at all.

A puppy can bring new life to an older dog—just introduce them carefully and respect your senior dog's feelings.

The Roles of Family, Friends, and Foes

✴ Please do not try and figure out who the "alpha" is and give that dog special privileges, because you could be wrong. Many folks give that honor to the wrong dog, simply because they don't have a background in canine behavior, so they didn't really know what to look for. For example, if you have a dog that steals all the toys, runs to you first for attention, or eats first, that doesn't mean he's the alpha. He could be an "alpha wannabe," and giving that dog special privileges over your other dogs could upset the pack more than help it. Instead, *you* be the alpha. Teach all your dogs manners and you get to decide all the rules for the team.

✴ Many puppies love to chase cats, and cats don't make it easy for you to train your puppy, either. They'll wait until your puppy is nice and calm then speed across the dining room, with targets practically flashing on their backs. Your puppy just can't resist the temptation to give hot pursuit. If this is a problem you're having, keep your puppy on a leash and teach him to "Leave it." This means you have to make a really big deal about your puppy leaving the cat alone, since the desire to chase is so strong. If you're trying to reward your puppy with a mere "Good dog!" in exchange for ignoring a moving cat, it's like giving up chocolate cheesecake for a piece of dry toast. Not much comparison, huh? Go nuts, praise like crazy, grab the nearest puppy toy and play with your puppy as a reward for leaving the cat alone. Practice, practice, practice and make it more exciting for your puppy to leave the cat alone than to chase it.

Just as you teach your puppy to be gentle around your cat, make sure your cat is gentle around your puppy. Cats have been known to bite puppies or swat at their eyes and cause damage. Make sure your cat feels safe so that he won't feel like he needs to protect himself. It helps

When Sibling Rivalry Turns Dangerous

Dogs will have spats from time to time, and generally all parties come through it without a scratch. But sometimes dogs do not get along and can seriously hurt each other. This shouldn't be a surprise to us, because we don't like everyone we meet, do we? We're not usually forced to live with someone we can't stand. But it does hurt, because you love all your animals and you want them to get along.

If your dogs are doing damage to each other, don't wait. It will not get better by itself, and you don't want a trip to the emergency vet clinic. Call in a professional dog trainer to assist you. There may be exercises that can help or management tools you can use. Ultimately, you may have to face the difficult decision of rehoming one of your pets. Whatever you decide, a professional can help you find the best and safest course for all your family—humans and canine alike.

to put up a few baby gates around the house. The cat can jump over them to safety, but the puppy can't.

Puppies love the taste of cat poop. It's disgusting, but not unusual. Cats don't really appreciate puppies getting into their litterboxes, either. Use good management and just put the litterbox away or up where your puppy can't reach it. This will disappoint your puppy, but you'll rest easier the next time he kisses you.

In general, you can help make your existing pet happier about your new addition if only good things happen when your puppy is around. Give your older dog special treats only when the puppy is in the room, and then make the treats disappear when the puppy leaves. Do this over and

The Roles of Family, Friends, and Foes

Instead of trying to figure out which dog is "dominant," you take over the role of leader and teach all your dogs good manners.

over and your older dog will soon start associating the puppy with the yummy treats. You can also do this with cats. Just find a treat your cat really loves; it can even be a small bite of wet cat food. Scoop some food onto a spoon and give your cat little tastes of it when the puppy walks by. When the puppy moves away, take the spoon away. You can even get a family member or friend to help you. They can lead the puppy in the room on leash and then lead him away so you can better control your training session.

Make sure you give all animals equal love time as individuals, set common rules they all have to follow, and you're on your way to a happy family.

Tools for Success

Now that you better understand why your puppy is acting outta control, how do you fix the problem? Many owners want their puppies to *stop* doing things. "Stop chasing the cat!" "Stop running away from me when I'm trying to get you to come inside!" "Stop jumping on me!"

There's a problem with this approach: It's very hard to teach the *absence* of a behavior; to teach your puppy the general concept of "stop doing whatever it is you're doing right now that is annoying me." That's a human concept that's rather broad and a bit complex for a puppy brain. Plus, puppies are bundles of young energy. If they stop doing one thing, heaven knows they'll just start doing something else. Now, wouldn't it be great if you could use this to your advantage? You can.

Stop Those Behaviors by Starting Here

Let's analyze the general issue in basic terms. Your dog is doing something you don't like. You want your dog to do *something else*—something you like—instead. Once you understand this concept, you've got a whole world open to you, one that is much easier to communicate to your puppy.

Think of all the things your puppy is doing that make you unhappy. You may have quite a long list. It's frustrating, isn't it? Well it's time to feel better, because for every behavior your puppy does that you don't like, there are *many* alternate behaviors you can teach him to do instead.

For example, let's say your puppy goes bonkers when the doorbell rings and scares the living daylights out of your guests. What things would you rather him do instead? You could teach him:

* To sit politely for treats from your guests instead of jumping on them.
* To grab his favorite toy and hold it in his mouth, to muffle his barking.
* To run into his crate.
* To lie down on his bed.
* To run into the kitchen, open the fridge, and get your guest a can of soda.

Okay, so we're not going to cover that in this book, but are you getting the picture? You *can* teach your dog that trick, and it's a heck of a lot better than mauling your guests.

There are *lots* of things you can teach your puppy to do that are acceptable behaviors. Start substituting the choices in your mind. Once you start looking at training this way, you see it's not hopeless at all. There's a world of possibilities for you.

Is it work? Oh yes, hard work. Unfortunately, there is no magic pill or wand to "poof" the problems away. You will have to communicate with your puppy in terms he can understand. You will have to be patient and consistent and have excellent timing. Training your dog will be work, but the effort you put into it will pay off for the both of you.

For every puppy behavior you don't like, you can teach an alternative behavior that you do like. For example, teach your dog to sit instead of jumping up.

It's an empowering venture; you get just as much out of it as you put into it. The more you work with your puppy, the more results you'll see, and the results will be a trained, happy dog that won't embarrass you in front of your friends or give you nightmares about appearing with him in public. Wouldn't that be a dream? You can do it.

A Good Leader Is a Great Manager

Many puppy problems can be solved by something so simple that many people overlook it: Management; solid management of the situation.

Let's say Fido loves to get into your trashcan. You could come home to the lovely sight of trash all over your house (usually when you're expecting company, of course) and be irritated and angry at your dog, or you could manage the problem:

* Put a lid on the trashcan that he can't open.
* Put the trashcan in a pantry or other place where he can't reach it.
* Crate him during the day when you're gone so he never has the chance to go near it in the first place.

There you go—three management solutions right there, all resulting in your coming home to trash in the trashcan, where it belongs. You won't be angry at your puppy for doing something wrong, because he never had the *chance* to do anything wrong at all.

These puppies can't knock over the garbage if the lid is on tightly. Many problems can be solved simply by anticipating your puppy's actions and managing the situation properly.

Remember, every time your dog performs a behavior you don't like, it's giving him a chance to practice that behavior. Everyone knows that practice makes perfect! If you manage the situation so he *can't* perform the "bad" behavior, he won't get good at it. Instead, set your puppy up to succeed. You're going to teach your pup behaviors you like and give him lots of rewarding opportunities to practice those behaviors instead. Think about the things your outta control puppy does that drive you crazy—are there

Teach your dog behaviors that you approve of and give him plenty of rewarding opportunities to practice those behaviors.

ways you can deal with them with good management? Here are a few common challenges.

❋ *My puppy pesters my guests when they come over. He's obnoxious, begging for attention!*

Put your puppy up before your guests even walk in the door. Crate your puppy or confine him so he can't bother your guests. When things settle down a bit, bring your puppy out on leash so you can better control the situation. Practice your obedience and use the visit as a training opportunity. For example, ask your guests to *only* pay attention to your puppy when he sits politely. If he gets up, they should ignore him. Puppies do what works. Soon, he'll learn the only way to get attention is to sit.

❋ *My puppy can hold it all day, but she has accidents at night when I'm asleep. I'm tired of waking up to poop on the floor.*

If your puppy is eliminating in the house at night, then she shouldn't be loose at night. Otherwise, you're just giving her the chance to practice unwanted behavior and learn a bad habit. If you can't supervise her, confine her until she's housetrained.

✴ *My puppy bolts out the door, and I have to chase him all over the neighborhood.*

This is dangerous, because a car could easily hit your puppy if he's running loose and outta control. Block off the door so your puppy does not have access to that room. If your house's layout does not allow you to do this, make sure everyone in your family knows to put the puppy in a secure place, like his crate, whenever they open the door. This is how to manage the situation until you train your puppy not to run away from you.

Confining your puppy to a safe area when you can't supervise him takes away the possibility that he will get into trouble.

Your Outta Control Puppy

Most puppies respond very positively to treats and are motivated to perform when food is involved. It's a paycheck for good behavior.

Tools for Success

Here are some tools you will need to start getting your puppy under control.

* **Treats:** We all work for paychecks, so why should dogs be any different? Treats are your dog's paycheck. They should be very small—your puppy only needs a taste of something yummy to perform. Just because you use treats, it doesn't mean you have to carry hot dogs in your pockets for the rest of your life. You can gradually wean off the treats as your puppy better understands what you want.

* **Praise:** Use a happy voice.

* **Leash:** Get a four- to six-foot cotton or nylon leash to work with your dog. Retractable leashes are convenient for exercising your

dog, but they are not as easy to hold as regular leashes and can be cumbersome.

✳ **Collar:** With reward-based methods, there's no need for old-fashioned choke chains or prong collars. Instead, use a regular, flat, nylon, quick-snap or buckle collar. You should just be able to fit two flat fingers between your puppy's neck and collar—any more and your puppy might wriggle out of it.

✳ **Specialty collars:** If you have a narrow-necked puppy, like a Greyhound or Doberman, you may find a martingale collar fits the bill. If you have a bad puller or jumper, you may find a head halter to be an extremely convenient tool. It's like power steering, and there's not any pressure on your dog's trachea, unlike choke chains or prong collars. Be sure the head halter is fitted properly. If you have questions, consult a professional dog trainer or veterinarian.

A good adjustable collar and a six-foot leash will help make it much easier to train your puppy.

Introducing the Head Halter

Do you wear glasses? Remember the first time you put them on, how funny and irritating they felt on your nose? If you just slap a head halter on a puppy and go, it's likely to annoy him, too. You need to introduce the head halter gradually and make it a pleasant experience.

* Hold the nose loop open and lure your puppy's nose through the loop with a treat. When his nose goes through, give him the treat and praise. Repeat several times. It may take a day or two for him to get the concept, and that's okay. Always quit leaving your puppy wanting more.

* When your puppy loves pushing his nose through the nose loop, it's time for the next step. This time, snap the collar on, give him several treats right in a row, then take off the collar. Repeat a couple times, then take a break.

* When your puppy tolerates the collar well, start feeding him every meal while he wears the collar. Remember, the head halter is not an everyday collar— your puppy should not wear it unsupervised or he could get caught up in something.

* Take your puppy for short walks in his head halter. Keep treats with you and praise him for polite behavior. If he paws at the nose loop, just gently pull up your leash and walk a bit faster. Praise him when he leaves the nose loop alone.

When your puppy learns the head halter is associated with all his meals and fun walks, he will learn the head halter is a good thing.

* **Your time:** The time you spend with your puppy, playing, petting, and training, makes a significant impact on your puppy's behavior. The more time you spend, the more work you are putting into making your puppy a better companion.

✳ **Toys:** Chew toys, like Nylabones®, can help redirect your puppy's energy and give him a constructive chewing alternative. Toys also help allieviate boredom and can keep your dog occupied and out of mischief.

Management Headquarters: The Crate

It's not a jail, it's not a cruelty—it's a crate. Dogs are den animals, and so are we, for that matter. If you think about it, we live in crates, too—big boxes we call houses. We get in a small crate with tires and drive to a bigger crate to work during the day, then get back in the small crate with tires to drive to our house crates at night. We adjust fine to our crates, and your puppy can, too.

When it comes to management tools, the crate is your puppy's headquarters for learning proper household behavior and keeping safe. Think of it as a playpen for an active puppy; a playpen that can help you

Traveling with your puppy is much safer and easier with the Nylabone® Fold Away Pet Carrier.

Your Outta Control Puppy

manage your puppy's behavior while you're working to train him.

Crate Advantages

The crate is your puppy's headquarters for learning proper household manners and keeping safe.

❄ They are safe places for young, active puppies. Leaving a puppy loose in a household is like leaving a two-year-old human child loose in a house when you go to work. Puppies are no different. They can get into all sorts of trouble if left alone to run loose, and they can get seriously hurt.

❄ Puppies chew—they can't help it, that's what puppies do. Sometimes they chew things that can hurt them. You can replace your couch, shoes, cabinet corners, even wallpaper, but you can't replace your precious puppy if he electrocutes himself by chewing on wires. It's important to confine your puppy when you can't watch him every second. If a puppy is crated when you are at work, he can't chew on anything that can hurt him.

❄ Housetraining your dog is much easier with a crate. Puppies generally don't soil their dens, so your pup will learn to "hold it" better if confined to a crate. However, please be fair. Remember, young puppies have young bladders. A common rule of thumb is to take your puppy's age in months and add one for the total number of hours she can stay in her crate without having to potty. This also depends on your breed. Toy breeds and other small dogs generally have to potty more frequently, so decrease the amount of time for those pups. In general, if your pup is four months old, add one, which equals five hours, which is the most she should stay in the crate without a potty break.

* Crates are a safe place to keep your puppy when you have activities going on in your home. The cable guy on his way? The plumber coming to fix the washer? Rather than having a puppy underfoot, a crate is a much safer alternative.

* Traveling with your puppy is safer and easier with a crate. Once you get your puppy under control, you're going to want to take him everywhere with you. Your friends and family might feel better about having your puppy in their homes if he is crate trained. In a strange environment, he'll feel safer in his familiar den. He can't destroy a hotel room if he's in a crate, and he can't escape when the maid ignores your "Do Not Disturb" sign and opens your hotel room door.

Puppies love to chew and can get into dangerous situations if not supervised. A crate and some chew toys will help keep your puppy out of trouble.

* There may come a time when your puppy has to stay overnight at the vet's or groomer's. They are not going to give your pup the

Taking Your Pup On the Road

Whether you have an outta control puppy or an older angel dog, your pets should be confined when traveling in your car. If they get in your way, they can cause an accident and can be seriously hurt or even killed. Just as children ride in car seats, your canine kids should be kept safe, too. Put your dog's crate in the car and secure it with a seatbelt or bungie cords. If your car is not big enough to accommodate the crate, get a dog seatbelt, which is a harness that secures to your car seat belt. If you have front seat, passenger-side airbags in your vehicle, be sure to secure your puppy in the backseat.

Please, never let your puppy ride with its head out the window or loose in the back of a pickup truck. Your pup may love it, but as your dog's guardian, it's up to you to keep him safe. Dogs' eyes often get cut by flying debris, and you would never forgive yourself if your puppy was thrown out of the back of your truck. If you have a truck and need your dog to ride in the back, get a crate and secure it firmly, then let your pup ride inside in safety and comfort.

run of the clinic or shop. They are going to crate him, and if he's familiar with a crate, this will not be as traumatic for him.

With all these advantages, is there ever a downside to using a crate? The most common problems are:

* Leaving a puppy in the crate all the time. That's not management, that's avoiding the issue. Be sure your puppy has plenty of quality time, exercise, and affection outside his crate.

* Using the crate as punishment. The crate should be a safe den for your puppy; a place he will want to go when he's sick, tired, or needs to rest. Never yell at your puppy and toss him in his crate to punish

him. If you do, then he will start dreading the crate, and you will lose all its benefits. You *can* use the crate for timeouts, but it should always be done calmly and without anger. If your puppy is crashing through your home with the puppy zooms or is pestering the cat into early senility, just calmly take him to his crate, put him in, and ignore him for about five minutes. What you are doing here is taking away his right to be loose as a direct consequence of his behavior.

* Letting children play in the crate. Many kids like to play "fort" in crates, but this is not a good practice. If your puppy needs a break from the kids and goes to rest in his den, he could feel threatened and trapped if they loom in the door or crawl in there with him. You don't want any dog bites. And how safe and secure could a crate be to a puppy if he sees children playing in and out of it? If you have kids in your life, please teach them to respect your puppy's "house" and to not play in or around it.

Never use the crate as punishment—your puppy should think of his crate as a happy place to retreat and relax.

Your Outta Control Puppy

If you do not wish to crate train your puppy, block off a puppy-proofed area of your house to place him in when you are not home.

✳ Some folks prefer to confine their puppy to a specific room in the house, usually a bathroom, kitchen, or laundry room, instead of getting a crate. It's better than leaving your puppy loose, but just make sure he isn't able to practice unwanted behaviors. For example, if your puppy is pottying in the room when you're gone, he's practicing pottying in the house. If he's rounding off every corner of your kitchen cabinets, then he's practicing chewing on items you'd prefer left alone. Puppies have been known to even chew their way through bathroom doors. That's not the plan for success we're aiming for, so evaluate your situation and see which approach works best for you.

Crate Basics

Now that you understand the importance of managing your puppy with a crate, what kind of crate should you get? There are so many to choose

Make sure you get a sturdy crate that will be big enough for your puppy as he matures.

from: wire ones, plastic ones, collapsible ones, expensive ones that match your household décor—it's a confusing choice. The Nylabone® Fold Away Pet Carrier is a good choice because it folds up for easy storage when not in use.

Puppies chew, so be sure to get a sturdy crate. If housetraining is a problem, a crate should be just large enough for your puppy to stand up, stretch out, and turn around in. If the crate is too big, then your puppy will be able to potty in a corner and stay high and dry, which is not the plan. What if you have a puppy that's going to grow into a large dog? Does this mean you have to get different sized crates as he grows? You can block the back of the large-sized crate with a box or wood, but many puppies will just chew it. Instead, get a divider that allows you to limit the size of the crate and increase it as your puppy grows. This way you can make one investment in a full-size crate for when your puppy is grown, but still limit your dog's area while you're housetraining. The crate grows as your puppy does.

Don't be surprised if you bring home a wonderful crate for your puppy, and he doesn't want anything to do with it. If your puppy has always been allowed to run loose and do whatever he wants, there's no way he's going to understand why you suddenly changed the rules and locked him up in prison. You need to teach him that his prison is really a palace.

Step 1: Preparation

1. Put the crate where your puppy will be near your family. The goal is not to banish him from your kingdom, just to manage that little jester's antics when you are not able to watch him.

2. Think of a cue to use when your puppy goes into his crate and use it every time he goes in. "Go to kennel," "Kennel up," or "Go to bed" work, but it doesn't matter what cue you use, just make sure you (and your family) use the same cue for this specific action every time.

3. When should your pup be in his crate? Whenever you can't watch him like a hawk to make sure he isn't practicing behaviors you don't like. If you are at work, he should be in his crate. If you are preparing dinner and can't watch him to make sure he doesn't have an accident, then he should be in his crate. It does seem like a lot of time at first, but as your puppy gets older and under better control, then he'll be able to spend more and more time out of his crate.

Start crate training gradually. Begin by feeding your puppy in his crate and rewarding him when he stays in for short periods of time.

Step 2: Training

1. Start gradually; don't just toss your puppy in there and shut the door. This might make him fear the crate. Build up slowly. It might be a good idea to start training on a weekend so you have more time to help your puppy get used to his new den.

2. First, leave the crate open and toss some treats in there when you pass by throughout the day. Let your puppy go in after the treats, and when he does, praise him, "Good puppy!" Don't shut the door behind him yet.

3. For all his meals: Get his meal ready, put the bowl in the crate and shut the door, with the puppy *outside the crate*. Wait about five minutes for him to build up some anticipation, then let him in the crate with his cue, "Go to kennel!" Let him eat his meal without shutting the door behind him.

Step 3: Reinforcement

1. If your puppy is now eagerly going into his crate, you are ready for Step 3. If he still resists, spend some more time on Step 2. If you push your puppy too fast, that will undo all your hard work.

2. Get a treat in your hand. Show it to your puppy and give him the cue, "Go to kennel!" (or whatever cue you have chosen). Then use the treat in your hand to lure him into the crate. If he follows right on in, give him the treat when he gets into the crate and praise him. Do this several times a day. If he does not follow the treat lure into the crate, go back to Step 2 for a while, and then try again—except this time, use better treats.

3. Now that your puppy is happily going into his crate, start shutting the door for a few minutes, then let him out when he's being quiet

and not barking or pawing at the door.

4. Gradually increase the time your puppy stays in his crate. Start with a few minutes, then a half hour, then an hour. Make sure to give him plenty of breaks in between your crate training sessions.

5. Gradually work up to longer times in the crate.

If your puppy goes into his crate eagerly, give him a treat and praise him.

Be sure to vary your routine; sometimes leave him in the crate when you are home and just puttering around the house instead of always when you leave. Otherwise, your puppy may start associating the crate with you leaving, and that could make it a negative experience.

Step 4: Advanced Training

1. By now your puppy is running into his crate when you give him the cue and staying in there for appropriate amounts of time. He's not? Then go back to Step 3 and work some more until you're ready to move onto Step 4.

2. Now it's time to stop using a cookie to lure your puppy in his crate. Instead, give him the cue, "Go to kennel!" and point to his crate as if you have a cookie in your hand. This is not to fool your puppy. Dogs are now being trained to smell cancer; they can tell when you have and when you don't have a cookie in your hand. What you are doing is using the same hand signal you've actually been teaching

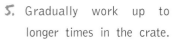

It may take time for your puppy to get used to his crate, but it will be worth it.

your puppy all along. Dogs learn body language much faster than verbal language. If you use your hands the same way, your puppy will better understand what you want of him. As soon as he goes in the crate, say "Good puppy!" shut the door, and quickly get a treat from where you keep them and give it to him through the crate door. This will teach your puppy that you don't always have treats with you, but he should still do what you ask because he'll be rewarded.

Running into trouble? Here are some common challenges.

✳ *When I go to let my puppy out of his crate, he freaks out and starts whining and pawing at the door.*

Don't let this pay off. Never let your puppy out of his crate if he's whining, barking, crying, or pawing at the door. Just wait him out; don't yell at him, don't say anything. Implement the easiest of training techniques—the Art of Doing Nothing. Just ignore him. He will see that his behavior is not getting you to do what he wants and he will eventually stop. When he does, reach for the door. Be careful, because as soon as you do he probably will start acting up again, but just stop and ignore him again.

Your Outta Control Puppy

Your puppy is smart. If you let him out when he's being obnoxious, then he'll learn that's what it takes to get you to open the crate door. Instead, teach him that if he barks, cries, or acts like a brat, you turn into a statue and ignore him. If he's quiet and sweet, he gets to come out of his crate. The first time you try this it might take a couple attempts before you actually get the door open. That's fine. If you are consistent, the next time will be quicker, and the time after that even faster, and so on.

❋ *My puppy cries in his crate.*

Has your puppy been in the crate too long? If you have a five-month-old puppy and he's been in a crate for nine hours, his whining may be a signal he has to potty. But if your puppy has not been in his crate too long, then he's probably just frustrated or a bit stressed. If he has never been crate trained, this is a new experience for him. The more you teach him the crate is a place where wonderful things happen—meals, treats, toys—the more he will realize his new experience is a pleasant one.

In order to make crate training a success, the crate should be an enjoyable place to be.

Don't yell at your puppy if he cries or barks—to a puppy, that's just joining in. Just ignore him. Stock up on your patience, and you can get through this together. Remember, if you let him out of his crate when he whines, then that's teaching him that whining works.

✳ *Forget whining, my puppy screams in his crate all night. I can't get any sleep!*

Oh, these are the hard ones. There are a few puppies who bark, scream, and wail about being in a crate, and it makes for a miserable experience for all involved. But you *can* get past it. It takes tons of patience and consistency, and earplugs are not a bad option, either.

First of all, where is the crate? Sometimes putting the crate in your bedroom helps, because your puppy feels more secure near you. Then again, it also can put you nearer to the clamor.

If you only let your puppy out of his crate when he is silent, he will know that whining or crying will not liberate him.

Crate Safety

❄ Take your puppy's collar off when he's in a wire crate, because it could get caught and hurt or strangle him.

❄ Put your puppy's favorite, safe toys in the crate with him. Do not leave him in his crate with toys that require supervision. If you don't know what kind of toys are safe for an unsupervised puppy, please consult your veterinarian or dog trainer.

❄ If your puppy is a chewer, don't leave blankets, beds, or other easily destroyed items in his crate. Some puppies will shred them to bits, which is bad enough, but some will eat them. It may seem kind of barren to not have a soft place for your puppy to lie on, but it's better than emergency surgery to remove a blankie from his stomach.

Right before bedtime, it also helps to play hard with your puppy and get him good and tired. Be sure he goes potty right before going into his crate. If your puppy is not a destructive chewer, then put one of your old T-shirts—one you have worn and not washed yet—into his crate with him. Having your smell near him may also comfort him.

The rest of the process usually takes about a full week or so to get through. You're going to have to go against everything you want to do and do nothing. Resist the overwhelming human need to yell at your puppy, because that will make it worse. He won't shut up, and you'll just be adding to the noise. Scream into your pillow if it helps. Don't smack the top of his crate or spank him; that will just add to his stress. Instead, as your eyes grow heavy and bleary with lack of sleep, listen for the silences. Your puppy has to breathe sometimes. When he does, the

It is hard to resist indulging your adorable puppy, but remember that setting up consistent rules now will help curb bad behavior later.

instant that he does, soothingly purr, "Goooooooood puppy." Yes, he will go right back to screaming again, but your puppy is smart. If you are consistent, he will learn to be quiet and that screaming isn't getting him anywhere. If you give up, even just once, you are just undoing all your training so far.

Why put up with all that screaming if the dog is truly stressed? Is it worth crate training a dog if he's that upset? Sometimes, as a pet owner, you have to make these difficult decisions. You may not always make decisions your dog likes, for his own good. Is your dog having accidents in the house? Being destructive? What would the consequences be if he were loose instead of crated? Could he eat something that would hurt him? Only you can decide if the risks are worth taking.

✳ *I put a blanket in my puppy's crate for her comfort but she pees on it. I'm sick of doing puppy laundry every day.*

Aaah, the puppy who's learned she can pee on her blanket, ball it up in a corner, and stay dry. Smart puppy, but you can be smarter. Just take the blanket away from her. She can earn the right to have it back when she stops peeing in her crate.

Practical Solutions to Pesky Problems

It's time to get down to the real problems. Your puppy is sweet and adorable, but she has some seriously annoying habits. She's nowhere near to being that loyal, pleasant companion you pictured when you decided to get a dog. You need help, and you need it fast. This is the chapter for you.

Housetraining

Your carpet is a disaster. You're afraid to walk around barefoot for fear of what you'll step in. The worst thing is that you give your puppy plenty of time to go outside, and the first thing she does when she comes in is pee on the floor. What is up with that?

The problem is not really housetraining—it's communication. Puppies are not born knowing to potty outside your home. You have to teach them. But you thought you made it obvious to him, right? Well, what you thought you were teaching your puppy probably wasn't what he understood.

You let your puppy outside and think, "I want my puppy to pee and poop outside." What your puppy thinks is, "Woo hoo! It's time to party! Look! There's the neighbor. And some leaves. And the garden hose to chew on."

Many owners experience housetraining problems with their puppies; however, with a regular schedule and lots of supervision, any healthy dog can be housetrained.

There are far too many distractions for your puppy outside; it's like turning a child loose in a theme park. Then when your puppy comes inside, the environment is not as exciting, so he remembers he has to pee. That's why your carpet suffers, despite the fact your puppy spent an hour outside.

You have to explain the concept of eliminating outside to your puppy in terms he can understand. By the same token, you can't expect your puppy to always let you know in obvious

Make sure your puppy has plenty of opportunities to eliminate outside in order to avoid accidents in the house.

terms when he has to eliminate. Some people complain that their dogs don't bark or paw at them to let them know they need to go outside, but how can a dog know that's what you want if you haven't taught it? Your puppy may be giving you lots of signals that you don't pick up on. He may be thinking, "I've been staring at my human for 20 full seconds now and she *still* doesn't understand I need to go. Humans are so dense sometimes."

In order to successfully housetrain your puppy, you both need to be on the same page. First, avoid these common mistakes.

* Having unrealistic expectations of how long puppies should be able to "hold it." Puppies under the age of about four months do not even realize they have to go ahead of time. One minute they're zipping along happily and then—oops! Just went! Be patient and remember that your puppy is still a baby, and babies

As a responsible dog owner, you should always clean up after your dog, both inside and out.

simply do not have the physical control of adults. If you get frustrated, just think how much longer it takes to housetrain human children.

✳ Punishing puppies after finding an accident. If you catch your puppy actually eliminating in your house, you can effectively use a verbal, "No!" to communicate to him you don't like that behavior. Then immediately rush him outside to finish so you can praise him. However, if you are hours, minutes, or even seconds away from catching him in the act—you're too late. Physical punishment will not teach him anything except not to trust you. After all, eliminating is a natural animal behavior. Spanking your puppy or rubbing his nose in his mess will not explain to your puppy you want him to potty outside. Instead, you could accidentally teach your pup to hide his messes in order to avoid your anger. That's how you end up with poop under the couch.

✳ Not cleaning up the mess with the right cleaner. Many puppies will visit the same spot and eliminate again and again, because the spot smells like previous accidents. Using vinegar or carpet cleaners will make the area smell great to humans, but puppies can still smell their scent through the floral freshness. Pet-specific cleaners have special enzymes to break down odors at the source, so your puppy will be less likely to return to the scene of the crime.

✳ Confusing the issue with paper training or puppy pads. It's easy to teach a puppy a few basic black-and-white concepts: "Outside is great for pottying. Inside is not." If you introduce an intermediary step, you're making it harder for your puppy to understand what you want. By using paper, you are now telling him: "Outside is great for pottying. Inside is not, unless it's on a certain surface I want you to use." If you teach your puppy it's okay to eliminate on newspapers or puppy pads, you're saying it's okay to eliminate in the house. You can't be mad at your pup later if she pees all over the newspaper issue you haven't read yet. How is a puppy supposed to know recycled newspaper from breaking news? Also, many puppies would rather shred puppy pads than pee on them. If you only want your dog to eliminate outside, it's much easier to teach that concept from the start.

Paper training can sometimes confuse puppies. If you want your puppy to eliminate outside, teach him that from the start.

Practical Solutions to Pesky Problems

✳ Giving the puppy too much freedom, too soon. If your puppy is not housetrained, then it should not be loose, unsupervised, or you're just giving him a chance to practice eliminating in the house.

Housetraining your puppy is truly not complicated, but it does take great patience, consistency, and diligence on your part. The results are worth it—just think of all the carpet cleaner you'll save.

Step 1: Preparation

1. Feed your puppy on a regular schedule. Do not free feed your puppy, which means leaving food down all the time. Free feeding is not as healthy for your puppy as regular meals. It's harder to control your puppy's weight if food is down all the time, and it can wreck your housetraining attempts. What goes *in* on schedule comes *out* on schedule. If you feed your puppy on a regular schedule, then you'll

Always feed and water your puppy at the same time every day and take him outside to eliminate immediately after.

Your Outta Control Puppy

Puppies Who Soil Their Crates

If your puppy soils his crate, the crate may be too big. However, if you got your puppy from a pet store, flea market, large volume breeder, or a puppy mill, you may have a special challenge on your hands.

A puppy's natural instinct is to eliminate away from where he eats and sleeps. At first, puppies may stumble just a few feet away and potty. But as their eyes open and get more coordinated, they travel a bit farther and eliminate away from their "dens." This wonderful, convenient instinct is built into puppies at birth, but it can be damaged and even destroyed by people.

Puppies who spend the first few weeks of their life in a cage cannot leave to eliminate. They have to potty where they live, because they can't move anywhere else. If the waste is not cleaned up immediately, which is unlikely in a busy store or large volume breeder setting, puppies learn to live with their waste all around them. Once they learn this sad acceptance at a tender age, it's very hard to train them otherwise.

You will have to be extra patient and extra vigilant to housetrain this type of puppy. Try using a larger crate or an ex-pen to give this puppy more room. Put in a litter box with live sod and encourage your puppy to eliminate on the sod. Give huge amounts of praise when this puppy eliminates outside. Just remember, your puppy did not have a choice about his start in life, so it's not his fault he never learned to be clean. You will just have to work harder to undo the damage someone else started, and your patient explanations in terms he can understand will help.

soon learn when your puppy has to eliminate. This will go a huge way toward establishing a housetraining routine. Consult your veterinarian for a feeding schedule, but in general, puppies six months of age and younger should eat three times a day, and older puppies and adults should eat twice a day.

Practical Solutions to Pesky Problems

During the housetraining process, keep a close eye on your puppy at all times, and if you must leave him unsupervised, confine him with a crate, ex-pen, or baby gates.

2. Take up your puppy's water in the early evening so he can better hold it during the night.

3. Confine your puppy if you cannot watch him like a hawk. This means using a crate, ex-pen, baby gates, etc. so he won't eliminate in the house. You can also "tether" the puppy to you with his leash so you can keep a better eye on him. The goal is to watch for signs that he has to eliminate, such as circling, sniffing, or whining, and prevent him from pottying in the house. If you are watching him closely, you can stop it before it happens.

Step 2: Training

1. Think of all the times your puppy has to eliminate. Generally, puppies have to potty when they wake up in the morning, after they eat, after they play really hard, after they wake up from naps, and every hour in between. Toy breeds and other small dogs have to go more frequently than larger dogs, because food and water don't have that far to travel through their little digestive systems. Also, puppies often have to go twice at a time, so in one five-minute session, they may pee and poop twice.

2. When you think your puppy has to eliminate, put him on leash. If your pup is on leash, you have better control over the situation. He

Your Outta Control Puppy

can't run around the backyard chasing butterflies and barking at the neighbors. Also, if you ever want to travel with your puppy, he will need to learn to eliminate on leash. Many dogs who have not been taught this never learn to have people near them when they eliminate, which creates an interesting dilemma at interstate rest stops.

3. Hide a treat in your hand. Take your puppy outside on leash and give him a cue that you will use only for this purpose, such as, "Go potty" or "Do your business." It doesn't matter what cue you use, just make sure you and your entire family only use it for this action.

4. Give your puppy about five minutes to eliminate. If you give your puppy a half hour, he'll learn he has a half hour to find a spot. Most people are busy and don't have time to follow their dogs around the yard for so long. You can teach your dog to eliminate quickly and on cue—it's just takes practice.

When your puppy does eliminate outside, praise him profusely and give him a treat.

Practical Solutions to Pesky Problems

Housetraining is important because it lets your puppy live with you as part of the family.

5. The second your dog eliminates, praise him like crazy and give him the treat. If your puppy does not eliminate, bring him inside and crate him for 15 minutes. Then try again.

6. Take your puppy inside. Watch him like a hawk and repeat the process, or, if you want your puppy to play in a fenced yard, then unhook his leash and give him a cue, like, "Go play." This will help him understand the difference between time to do his business and time to romp.

Running into trouble? Here are some common challenges.

✳ *What should I do if I catch my puppy peeing in the house?*

Oops! Chalk one up against you on the scoreboard! Every time your puppy has an accident in the house is one step backward in your housetraining, because he's had a chance to practice an unwanted behavior. While you're kicking yourself for not watching him more closely, shout a firm verbal, "No!," immediately leash your puppy, and rush him outside to finish. The very second he pees outside, praise him like crazy. Do not yell at him now, because eliminating outside is what you want. This is black-and-white communication: "Pottying inside makes me unhappy, but I *love* it when you potty outside." When he is finished, take him inside, confine him, and clean the mess with an enzymatic cleaner. Then watch him more closely next time.

❈ *My puppy used to be housetrained, but suddenly has started peeing everywhere.*

There are several reasons why formerly trained puppies can start eliminating in the house again. He could have a kidney or urinary tract infection, he may be on medication that causes him to pee more frequently, or he could be stressed by changes in his environment or routine. If your puppy is suddenly peeing in the house when he didn't before, please consult your veterinarian to make sure there isn't a physical problem. If your vet says your pup is okay, then start your housetraining back from scratch. Your pup just may need a refresher course.

Jumping

You have to brace yourself every time your puppy launches at you. You feel like a human trampoline. Maybe you have a large puppy and you're worried he may hurt someone by jumping.

Why do puppies jump up? Most likely, they want your attention. Even if you yell at them or push them away in irritation, that's still attention, so you may accidentally be rewarding the very behavior you want to get rid of. Using physical techniques, such as kneeing your puppy in

Most puppies jump for joy when they see you, but they must learn that jumping up on people will not be appreciated.

the chest or pinching his paws, will just teach your puppy to avoid jumping on people who are hurtful to him. What about Grandma or a toddler? Are they strong enough to knee your bouncy puppy? It's much easier to teach your puppy that keeping four paws on the ground is more rewarding across the board and that jumping never pays off.

Step 1: Preparation

1. Pick a cue to use for this specific action; for example, "Off." If you choose to use "Down" or "Get Down," just be sure you don't also use those terms for your puppy to lie down on the floor. One word should mean one specific action in training—it's too hard for your puppy to understand when one word means several things.

Step 2: Training

1. Put your puppy on leash. On leash, you have more control over the situation. Your puppy can't get bored with you and leave the room.

2. Hide a treat in your hand.

3. Implement a fun training tool—entrapment. Set your puppy up so he is likely to jump on you. Try jumping up and down excitedly.

Your Outta Control Puppy

4. When your dog jumps on you, calmly say your cue, "Off." Try hard not to say it in a harsh voice; this isn't discipline, it's communication. Fold your arms across your body. Turn your head to the side as if you are shunning him, but carefully peek out of the corner of your eye.

5. As long as your puppy is jumping or pawing at you, be patient. Don't say a word. Practice the training Art of Doing Nothing. Your dog will not receive the attention he craves, so sooner or later, he will quit and get off you. The very second he gets all four paws on the floor, praise and give him a treat. Hold the treat low to the ground so you're not luring him to jump up again.

6. If your puppy goes to jump again before he gets the treat, do not give it to him. Only give him the treat if four paws are on the floor. If you give him the treat while paws are in the air, it's rewarding that behavior.

Dogs do what works. When your puppy realizes that jumping isn't very rewarding, he may start sitting instead. If he does, *immediately* praise him and give him a treat.

When you ignore your puppy when he jumps up, you are teaching him that jumping is not a rewarding behavior.

Step 3: Reinforcement
What if your puppy is the type that goes nuts when the doorbell rings and jumps all over your guests? First, practice Step 2 until your puppy gets the picture, then you'll be ready for this step.

Practical Solutions to Pesky Problems

1. Get a friend or family member to help you train your puppy. Ask your friend to wait outside your front door.

2. Put your puppy on leash and hide a treat in your hand.

3. Have your friend ring the doorbell and wait for your puppy to go bonkers. Calmly open the door.

4. If your puppy jumps on your friend, your friend should fold her arms across her body and turn her head away as if she is shunning your puppy. You say, "Off" (or whatever cue you have chosen). Then you both wait; don't yell at your puppy, don't do anything except hold the leash so your puppy doesn't leave the training area.

5. Your puppy will soon realize that your friend isn't paying him any attention—how boring! The very second your puppy puts four paws on the floor, *you* praise and give him a treat.

If your puppy jumps on visitors, teach him to sit nicely by the door. Have your guests give him a treat when he shows good manners.

6. Your friend can now pet the puppy using a soothing, calm voice so as not to overexcite him. If your puppy jumps up, she should ignore him again.

7. Your friend should leave and do it all over again. After several repetitions, your puppy will soon learn that jumping is no longer rewarding for him, but staying on the ground is.

Your Outta Control Puppy

Running into trouble? Here are some common challenges.

Some people say that when my puppy puts his front paws in my lap and I pet him, that's the same as rewarding him for jumping. Is that true?

Be consistent when training your puppy. He will become confused if you let him jump on some people and punish him when he jumps on others.

They are on the money. If you pet your puppy for putting his front paws on you when you're sitting down, he won't understand why you don't like it just because you're standing up. Use your "Off" cue and only pet your puppy when four paws are on the floor. This is much clearer communication.

I have some friends who say they don't mind it when my puppy jumps on them. Is this confusing him?

Yes. If your puppy is allowed to jump on some people but not others, how is he supposed to understand the difference? Teach your friends to fold their arms and look away from your puppy when he jumps on them, while you give the cue, "Off." If they can't help you with your training program, then they don't get to play with your puppy.

Pulling on Leash

Do you walk your puppy or does your puppy walk you? Why do puppies pull on the leash? Well, they've already been where they are, so they're

Practical Solutions to Pesky Problems

You need to teach your puppy that pulling and yanking on the leash is not rewarding, but walking nicely next to you earns him praise and rewards.

excited to see where they haven't been yet. We need to teach your puppy that pulling is not rewarding but walking politely next to you *is*. First, avoid these common mistakes.

✱ Rewarding your puppy for pulling. Oh, you don't do that? Are you sure? Let's say you're walking your puppy down the street, and you see a good friend. Your puppy pulls you all the way to your friend, who showers him with attention. That's a reward for pulling. Does your puppy want to pee by the side of the road? If you let your puppy pull you to a spot, then he relieves himself, that's a reward for pulling. Make sure you aren't accidentally giving him a reward for this behavior.

✱ Using a retractable leash. Retractable leashes are great for exercising your dog, but they put a constant tension on your dog's collar. That can teach some dogs that there *should* be constant tension, instead of a loose leash.

Teaching your puppy to walk politely on a leash can be the hardest concept for some pups to grasp. It's going to take a lot of patience. You might be tempted to use harsh methods, thinking it will solve the problem more quickly, but that's not a long-term solution. It also has a lot of

Your Outta Control Puppy

negative side effects. Besides, you want your puppy to walk nicely with anyone, not just the person who can yank him back the hardest. For this exercise, you may find a head halter to be especially useful. It will help you get better control of your puppy until you can teach him what you want.

Step 1: Preparation

1. In your mind, imagine exactly where you want your puppy to walk next to you. Do you want him on your right side or your left? If you don't teach him a specific side, he could zigzag in front of you and trip you up. Do you want him right by your leg or maybe a little ahead of you? Think of the exact place you want your puppy as a picture frame. When he steps outside the frame, he's out of the picture you want.

2. Pick a cue to use for this specific action; for example, "Let's go" or "Let's walk." Make sure the words you use are only for this action.

Keep a treat in your hand and have your dog follow it while you walk. Praise him and give him the treat if he stays by your side.

Practical Solutions to Pesky Problems

3. At first, you should practice this exercise in a quiet area. It will be too much to ask your puppy to walk nicely by your side in a busy park. Start in a quiet environment, like your living room or backyard.

Step 2: Training

1. Put your dog on his leash and get him on the side of you that you want him to walk. If your dog knows "sit," ask him to sit.

2. Hold five small treats in your hand.

3. Give your cue, "Let's go," and start walking. For every step you take, give him a treat. This will seem very awkward at first, but just go slowly. You are teaching your dog that treats pour like rain when he walks next to you.

4. Practice this for one week, several times a day.

Step 3: Reinforcement

Now it's time to start weaning off the treats.

1. Put your dog on leash, get him on the appropriate side, and give your cue, "Let's go."

2. Instead of giving one treat for one step, take several steps before you give him a treat. If he loses interest, you're weaning off the treats too fast.

3. Watch your dog—where is he walking in your imaginary picture frame? If your dog walks perfectly where you pictured him to be, praise and treat every couple steps. If your dog lags behind, encourage him to keep up with you. Every time he comes up to

If your dog pulls on the leash, simply stop walking. Then show him you have a treat, lure him to your side, and have him sit.

your side, praise and give him a treat. If your dog *pulls*, stop walking. Show him you have the treat, lure him back to your side, and ask him to sit. Start over at the beginning of Step 3, except this time, don't walk as far. The goal is to have a nice walk for three steps, four steps, then more, gradually building toward success.

Step 4: Advanced Training

1. As your dog learns to walk nicely by your side, start gradually increasing the distractions in your environment; for example, go for walks around the block, to the park, or to a safe area in a store parking lot. You may have to back up a few steps at first, but your puppy will catch on if you are consistent. If you find your puppy is just too distracted, go back to a quieter place and gradually increase the distractions at a slower rate.

Practical Solutions to Pesky Problems

Running into trouble? Here are some common challenges.

✳ *My puppy walks okay on his leash, until he sees another dog. Then he goes bonkers and pulls me like a sled dog. What can I do?*

Even if you have come a long way in leash training, you may find some situations bring out the worst in your puppy. There may be things that are just more tempting to him and

Until your puppy is trustworthy, avoid distractions like other dogs and reward him for paying attention to you.

cause him to forget his training. Don't be stingy about using your treats in these instances. For example, you're walking in the park and see another dog and owner approaching. Quickly get out your treats and start feeding your puppy for paying attention to you. Move to the side of the path to keep the distraction as far away as possible and keep feeding your pup until the other dog passes. What have you done? You've just prevented your dog from practicing bad behavior—pulling you to get to the other dog—and rewarded him for paying attention to you instead.

✳ *Can I use a harness to teach my dog not to pull?*

Harnesses do not teach your puppy not to pull. Instead, they redistribute weight on your puppy to make pulling more efficient. Just think; they hook Huskies up to sleds with harnesses.

What a harness *can* do is protect your puppy's throat if he has a tracheal injury or problem, and you won't get that choking, hacking

Leaving the Leash Behind

Many folks want their puppies to follow them without having to attach a leash. Everyone knows at least one person with the perfect dog who never needs a leash and walks by his owner's side. This dog would stay right by his owner's leg despite kids offering hot dogs, squirrels running by, or tornadoes passing through.

The truth is that dogs who can successfully and safely walk off leash are the exception, not the rule. It takes years of careful training to get a dog to reliably walk next to you without being attached, and some dogs never accomplish it. Why? Because they're dogs.

Dogs are naturally curious. They want to investigate things, and every dog has at least one special motivation that may tempt it strongly enough that he will not do what you asked. It may be a child tossing a tennis ball, a cat dashing across its path, another dog making goo-goo eyes at it across the park—something will tempt him. It's unrealistic to expect all dogs to walk perfectly off leash, simply because of who they are.

Puppies, especially, easily fall into temptation. They are babies with no attention spans. They may happily trot by your side for a block and then dash off in hot pursuit of a butterfly.

Keep safe: If your puppy is not in a fenced yard, he should always be on leash. You would never forgive yourself if your puppy darted out into traffic or got hurt by another dog. Why take the chance? Get your puppy under control and master the basics first. Then, if you still want to explore off-leash walking, find a professional dog trainer to help you safely set your dog up for success.

noise your puppy might make when it pulls against a regular collar. A head halter can be an effective alternative and give you greater control. Then it's up to you to train your puppy not to pull.

Practical Solutions to Pesky Problems

Barking

Your neighbors are threatening action, and your ears ring from the constant racket. How were you supposed to know that little angel you brought home was so "talkative?" Some breeds, including some herding or toy breeds, are prone to barking. It's just in their genetic makeup. You may have brought home a dog that was destined to be a barker. (Oops, perhaps the breeder neglected to mention that?) Dogs also bark for different reasons:

* They are bored.
* They are protective.
* They are alerting you that's something is going on, although sometimes it feels like they're just telling you the grass is growing.

Even if you have a genetically predispositioned barker, you can help your puppy learn to be more quiet. Avoid these common mistakes.

Because they originally were bred to herd livestock or alert their owners to intruders, some puppies are more prone to barking than others.

* Rewarding the barking. You would never do that, right? Are you sure? Let's say your puppy barks like a maniac when you're getting his dinner bowl ready. It drives you nuts but you give him his food to shut him up. Guess what? You've just rewarded the barking. The next time you prepare his food, he'll bark *more*, because it worked so well last time.

* Yelling at your puppy to shut up. Ever notice how if one

The best way to treat a barker is to build his confidence and reinforce basic obedience.

dog starts barking, others in your home or neighborhood often chime in? That's what you're doing if you yell at your puppy. You may think, "I am obviously telling my puppy to be quiet," but your puppy is thinking, "Great! My owner is joining in. Let's bark together like the fierce pack we are!"

✳ Having unrealistic expectations for your puppy. Some people love it when their puppies bark when someone comes to the door, but then yell at their puppies when the barking goes on too long. How is your puppy supposed to know when enough is enough? You have to teach him.

Enough with the earaches; let's teach your puppy the wonderful sound of silence.

Step 1: Preparation

1. Pick a cue you will use to ask your puppy to be quiet. It can be "Hush," "Quiet" or whatever you want, just make sure you and your family use the same cue for this specific action, every time.

2. Think of a situation that will cause your puppy to bark, such as squeaking a toy or ringing the doorbell. By getting your puppy to make noise, you can then teach him the opposite action—silence.

Step 2: Training

Now it's time to teach your puppy the concept of quiet. This is the foundation you will use for later training, depending on why your puppy barks.

Praise your puppy as soon as he stops barking and give him a treat to show him that you will reward him when he's quiet.

1. Hide a tasty treat in your hand.

2. Do whatever action you've chosen to get your puppy to bark. After about three barks, give him your cue to "Hush." Try not to yell the word—remember, this is information, not correction.

3. Put the treat close or even touching his nose. He will stop to smell the treat—immediately praise and give him the treat. If he doesn't stop, that means your action was too exciting or the treat wasn't tempting enough (try steak!).

4. Repeat a couple times, then quit for the day. Repeat again tomorrow.

Your Outta Control Puppy

If your puppy barks because he is bored, give him lots of safe chew toys to keep him occupied.

With practice, your puppy will start barking a few times, then be quiet and start looking for his treat.

5. What if your puppy stops barking for his treat then starts right back up again after swallowing? When he starts barking again, immediately show him another treat, say "Too bad!" and turn your back and leave him. He'll learn he *doesn't* get treats if he keeps talking.

Step 3: Reinforcement

1. When your puppy reliably stops barking when you say your cue for quiet, then you can start weaning him off the treats. Do it gradually. Only progress as far as your puppy can succeed.

Now it's time to address the specific reason *why* your puppy is barking. Barking is often situational, so here are some common barking problems.

✳ *My puppy looks out the window and barks at people walking by. How can I stop this?*

Management may be your best solution. Close the curtains and block off the room so your puppy can't look outside. Yes, you may want her to enjoy the view, but is it worth her getting all worked up and causing so much noise? The more she barks, the more she's practicing barking, and the harder it will be to break the habit. Instead, give her exciting things to do inside—stuff some Rhinos® with food and make sure she gets plenty of exercise.

✳ *My puppy barks at other dogs and people. I think she's afraid of them.*

If your puppy hides behind you and barks, growls, or lunges, and barks

If you are consistently rewarding your dog when he is quiet, he will soon learn what is expected of him.

at people as they're moving away from her, she could be afraid. Never push your dog to meet a person or another dog if she is afraid, because it will only make her fear worse. Yelling or punishing her for barking will make her think there's a good reason to be afraid, since the sight of those other people or dogs cause her to be punished. Instead, find a reward-based professional dog trainer in your area and enroll the both of you in some classes or private training. Training will boost your dog's confidence, and in a reward-based class, she'll learn that strangers are not so scary after all.

Dogs bark for different reasons. When you discover why your dog is barking, you can help correct his behavior.

❋ *My puppy is outside all day when I'm at work and he barks at the neighbors. They're getting afraid of him. What can I do?*

Many outside dogs bark because they are bored. Invite your neighbors over and let your dog meet them, take treats from them, and know they are friends. Give your dog lots of praise when he is quiet around your neighbors. Increase your dog's exercise; just being loose in a fenced yard is not enough exercise for most dogs. Make sure your dog has interactive toys to play with, such as hollow toys like Rhinos® stuffed with food and safe toys like Nylabones® to chew on, and rotate the toys so he won't get bored. Enroll your dog in a reward-based training class to exercise his brain, too.

Practical Solutions to Pesky Problems

✳ *My puppy barks when someone comes to the door, which I like. But then he won't shut up!*

First, decide how long you want your puppy to bark. Two barks? Ten barks? Be consistent every time. When your puppy barks at the doorbell, rush to the door and thank him after he's barked your limit, "Good puppy!" Then tell him your cue for quiet and give him a treat when he's quiet, just like in the exercises we've outlined. By using only praise to thank him for barking, and using a stronger motivation, food, to get him to be quiet, being quiet will be more appealing to him.

It's also important to teach this exercise gradually, building up to harder situations. If your puppy has had a lot of practice barking too much at the door, it will be hard to start teaching him to be quiet the night you have a dinner party with 25 people arriving at the same time. A better way is to ask your guests to stagger their arrivals in five-minute increments. Put your puppy on leash for better control and use each guest's arrival as a training opportunity. By the time everyone gets there, your puppy will have had many chances to practice his new behavior.

✳ *My puppy barks for me to let him outside, fix his dinner, or basically to get me to do things for him. I can't stand the noise so I cave in. Is it too late to regain control without losing my hearing?*

It's not too late, but you will have to change *your* behavior before you can change your puppy's. Every time your puppy barks at you to do something, freeze and ignore him (here is where the training Art of Doing Nothing comes in handy again). Do not continue fixing his dinner, reaching for the door, or whatever it is he wants until he is silent. When he's quiet praise him, softly purring, "Gooooooood puppy," and start moving again. Yes, he will start right up barking, but every time he does, just freeze again.

The first time you do this will seem like it takes *forever*. But you're changing the rules, and habits are hard to break. The next time will be faster, and faster, and faster, if you're consistent and patient. Just wait it out. Your puppy is smart—he'll soon learn that if he's talking, you do nothing for him.

Illegal Use of Jaws: Chewing, Mouthing, and Stealing

You've paid a fortune replacing stuff because your puppy views the world as one big chew toy. You no longer have matching shoes, because for some reason, your pup only picks one of each pair to kill. There is not a doll in the house that doesn't live in fear of decapitation, and you feel like a giant pincushion. Is nothing safe from your Jaws on Paws?

Chewing and mouthing is a natural puppy behavior; however, it can be controlled and channeled into something appropriate.

Practical Solutions to Pesky Problems

Puppies chew because it feels good to their gums when they are teething. They chew when they are bored. They chew when they are stressed because it's comforting to them, just like reaching for that chocolate is comforting to us. They chew to play and because they are physically built to be good at it. In other words, chewing is a very natural dog behavior, but you can channel that behavior into something more appropriate. Here are some common mistakes to avoid.

✳ Letting your puppy run loose in your home when you can't supervise him. This just gives your puppy a chance to get into all kinds of trouble that can hurt him. A great solution is to manage the situation so that your puppy does not have a chance to destroy your household. Crate training can help significantly.

✳ Using physical punishment to try to get your puppy to stop chewing on you. Some folks try grabbing or pinching their puppy's muzzle or even poking a finger down their puppy's throat. It doesn't

Because puppies play very rough with each other, using physical punishment to stop your puppy from chewing does not work and may even encourage your puppy to bite harder.

Your Outta Control Puppy

take long to figure out the puppy just mouths back harder. This is because puppies play very rough with each other. (Ever watch two or more puppies roughhouse? They sound like they're killing each other.) When you use harsh methods, your puppy can think you are just upping the ante in the game. Even worse, it can make your puppy afraid of your hands. If it does happen to work and your puppy stops chewing on you, what about other members of your family? Are they all strong enough to use the same methods? It's much easier to teach your puppy to not chew on *all* people—not just the ones who are stronger than he is.

✳ Chasing your puppy when he steals something he shouldn't have and yelling at him when you catch him. Chasing is a great game to a puppy. He's the center of attention, until you catch him and take his prize away. That's no fun—it ends the game. Why should he shorten the game next time? He'll hold onto that prize even longer.

So how do you tame the jaws of your savage beast? Here are some different techniques, depending on how your puppy is putting those destructive teeth to work.

Chewing or Mouthing People

Puppy teeth *hurt*! One of the most valuable lessons you can teach your puppy is bite inhibition—human skin is very fragile and he shouldn't bite down hard upon it. Many pups learn this lesson as they grow up with their mom and littermates. If your puppy left his litter before the age of eight weeks or if he was an only child, then he may not have had a chance to learn this lesson very well. That means you have some catching up to do.

Most puppies wean from their mothers between three and four weeks of age, but this doesn't mean they're ready to leave the nest. As puppies play with each other, they learn bite inhibition. Little brother wrestles with little sister, and if he chomps down too hard, she yelps and ends the game. That's no fun, so little brother soon learns if he bites down too hard, he loses his playmate. This lesson is easiest taught with his canine family. You may not have known that when you got your puppy or you may have adopted your puppy as a rescue and have no idea at what age he left his litter. Either way, it's time to start bite inhibition training.

Step 1: Preparation

1. Get ready to do this exercise each and every time your puppy mouths you hard. If you skip it once or twice, then he won't learn it consistently.

Step 2: Training

1. When your puppy starts to mouth you, yelp, "Ouch!" like you've been severely wounded. Go for an acting award. Don't yell it like

you're mad (and you will be, because it hurts!). Instead, act like you are hurt.

2. Immediately turn your back for a few seconds and ignore the pup. Do not pay attention to him if he paws you, whines, or jumps at you. Don't ignore him for five minutes; a couple seconds is an eternity to a puppy.

One of the most valuable lessons you can teach your puppy is bite inhibition, because it will help him to socialize and play with people safely.

3. Turn back and find the nearest appropriate chew toy, give that to your pup, and praise heavily when he chews on that instead of you.

Your Outta Control Puppy

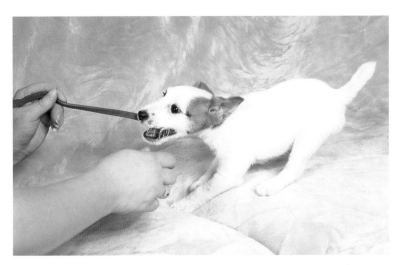

For a puppy, the fun of stealing something is the attention and play he gets when you try to take it back. You can teach him that it is rewarding to leave things alone when told.

4. You will have to do this dozens of times a day. It can become very frustrating, but don't give up. Remember, puppies have no attention spans, so he'll keep forgetting what you're trying to teach him. Don't worry—you *are* getting through to your puppy, even if you think you aren't. Just keep reminding him that every time he bites down hard, he loses his playmate, and one day the lightbulb will go off in his puppy brain.

Chewing and Stealing Stuff

You know about the benefits of crate training and how you should confine your puppy when you can't supervise him, but puppies are quick. What if he manages to nab something and run around the house with it playing "keep-away?" What if it's something dangerous?

Understand that puppies don't like to give things up because that usually ends the reward. But you can teach your puppy that leaving something alone *is* rewarding. This is where a strong "leave it" cue comes in mighty handy. This exercise is easy and fun to teach, and it can save your dog's life.

Step 1: Preparation

1. Pick a cue you will use to ask your puppy to leave something alone. It can be "Leave it," "Off," or whatever you want, just make sure you and your family use the same cue for this specific action, every time. For example, if you use "Off" to mean "Don't jump on you," you can't also use it to mean "leave something alone"—that's too confusing for your puppy.

Step 2: Training

1. Hide a treat in each hand and hold your hands a couple feet apart.

2. Open one hand, show your puppy the treat, and give the cue, "Leave it." Don't yell the cue—this is information, not a correction. Be sure the treat is at your dog's nose level, not high above his head or

When you take something away from your puppy, substitute it with something that he can chew, like a safe toy or a treat.

Your Outta Control Puppy

behind your back. The temptation should be right under your puppy's nose.

3. When your puppy goes for the treat, quickly make a fist so he cannot get it. It's important that your puppy not get the treat; however, don't keep your hand away from him; keep temptation right under his nose.

4. Be patient. Your puppy will probably lick your hand or paw at you. Don't say a word and don't move your hand away. Practice the training Art of Doing Nothing. If your puppy is really mouthing you hard and causing you pain, then you can fold your arm across your chest to hide your fist.

5. Your puppy will figure out that you are not going to release that treat, so sooner or later, he will offer another behavior. He will grow bored and look away, or he may even sit. It doesn't matter what he does, but the second he leaves your hand alone, praise him, "Good dog!" and give him the treat you had hidden in your other hand. Encourage him to walk away from the first treat to the one he gets as a reward. This will teach your puppy to turn his head away when you say, "Leave it," which could give you added seconds to get an object away from him in an emergency.

6. It's important your puppy give up temptation on his own, without any added assistance from you. Ask someone to watch your hands. Instead of waiting for your puppy to give up the treat on his own, are you actually luring him away with the "hidden" treat in your other hand? If so, sit on your hand or put it behind your back so that you won't be tempted to move it. Otherwise, you are just distracting your puppy and not teaching him to willingly leave something alone because you asked.

Practical Solutions to Pesky Problems

Step 3: Reinforcement

1. When your puppy is reliably leaving the treat alone in one hand, switch hands. For example, if you were asking him to leave the treat alone in your right hand and rewarding him with the left, ask him to leave the treat alone in your left hand and reward him with your right. Your puppy may regress, and that's normal. You changed the rules.

2. Practice this exercise in every room of your home, especially places where he is likely to steal things, like the kitchen and bathroom.

3. Practice this exercise outside in your yard.

Practice the "leave it" exercise in every room of your home, as well as outside with distractions.

Step 4: Advanced Training

1. Is your puppy responding to "Leave it" like a champ, in every room of your home and even outside? Then you're ready for Step 4. If not, go back a few steps and practice some more until your puppy is ready. If you push him too fast, you'll just undo all your hard work. This step will teach your puppy to leave things alone that get dropped on the floor.

2. Hide a treat in one hand.

3. Take a small, hard treat, one that won't mess up your carpet, and carefully drop it on the floor. Say, "Leave it," or whatever cue you have chosen.

4. Quickly cover the treat with your foot. It's important your puppy not get the treat. If you have to keep your puppy on leash to help with this, then that's okay.

5. Be patient. Your puppy will probably paw at your foot, but don't say a word. Practice the training Art of Doing Nothing.

6. Your puppy will soon figure out that you are not going to uncover that treat. Sooner or later, he will offer another behavior. He will grow bored and look away, or he may even sit. It doesn't matter what he does, but the second he leaves your foot alone, praise him, "Good dog!" and give him the treat you had hidden in your hand

7. Practice this exercise in every room of your home.

8. Practice this exercise outside your home.

Here is a common challenge.

 ✳ *My puppy likes to steal toilet tissue rolls or my kids' toys. How do I get him to leave them alone?*

Toyland

When picking chew toys, make sure you buy the right size and durability for your particular puppy. Never leave your puppy unsupervised with toys that break apart or that rip, like stuffed animals. Nylabones® are a very safe chewing alternative for your puppy. Also, rotate the toys—have an "A" team and a "B" team that are available to your puppy during alternating weeks. That way, every week he'll have "new" toys to keep his interest.

Practical Solutions to Pesky Problems

If your puppy likes to steal or chew specific items, then use those items as a temptation and train him to leave them alone. Replace them with safe toys that he is allowed to chew.

If your puppy likes to steal and chew on specific items, then use those items to train. Instead of using a treat as a temptation, just use the other item—toys, cardboard, pinecones, or whatever tempts your puppy. Now, some items will be too large to hide in your hand or cover with your foot. For these items, consider spending a few dollars on a plastic, clear cake dome. Drop the item on the floor and instead of covering it with your foot, cover it with the cake dome. Your puppy can't reach the item, but it will be in plain view. Follow the rest of the exercises as written.

The Insecure Puppy: Shyness

Your puppy loves you and your family, but every time people come over to your house, he runs and hides or barks at them from behind the furniture. When he does approach someone, he's low to the ground, maybe bobbing his head or lifting his paw, tail tucked, and generally looking miserable. Your friends think your dog is a wimp, and forget about taking him new places—he just cowers. It just breaks your heart to see him so afraid.

Some puppies are born shy. They may have had shy parents, a trait that passes down from parent to puppy. This is an especially difficult challenge. Although you can help these puppies be more comfortable in the world, you can't change their genes.

Some puppies are shy because they weren't socialized enough from the start. Maybe the breeder didn't let anyone interact with the puppies; maybe your puppy was a stray and never had the chance to learn that the world was a kind place. (Many folks who bring home rescues think their puppy has been abused in the past from the way it behaves. Actually, most of these puppies weren't physically hurt at all, they were just never exposed to new things. When you take them out into the world, it's a terrifying field trip.) Maybe you brought your puppy home and just didn't realize how much socialization your puppy would need to prevent problems later. Shyness does cause serious problems. Dogs can growl, snap, and bite out of fearfulness. Many times, aggressive behaviors have a root in fear.

Dealing with a shy puppy presents special challenges for you. We can't possibly cover all the nuances of living with a shy puppy here in this book, but we can offer you some first-aid tips. First, avoid these common mistakes.

Whether your puppy was born shy or just lacks socialization, you can help him feel more confident.

Practical Solutions to Pesky Problems

✳ Forcing a puppy to confront his fears. Let's say your puppy is scared of new people, so you pick him up and plop him in a friend's lap to prove that your friend is a kind person. You're thinking like a human. You figure you can reason with your puppy, "Just give it a try, Fido. I know this person is safe and you will learn to love her. See how kind she is?" Try a different perspective. To your puppy, that's not a friend—it's a stranger. From the puppy's point of view, you just broke his trust by plopping him down in the heart of danger. For example, let's say you are terrified of public speaking. The mere thought of talking to a group of people sends chills through your veins. One day, your best friend takes you for a ride and unexpectedly veers into the nearest conference center, grabs your hand, drags you into the building, and pushes you in front of 500 people who are waiting to hang on your every word. You are gripping the podium like a liferaft, looking at all those expectant

Dealing with a shy puppy can present challenges, but your patience, persistence, and training are key factors in helping your puppy.

Your Outta Control Puppy

faces waiting for you to speak. Do you feel cured? No way. You are more terrified than you were before, and now you're not real pleased with your best friend for this nasty trick, either. That's probably how your puppy feels when you force him to face his fear. There are much better ways to gradually help a puppy get confidence.

Training is one of the best ways to build your puppy's confidence and help him feel comfortable in new situations.

* Reassuring and petting your puppy when he is afraid. You are a caring puppy owner; otherwise, you wouldn't have bothered to purchase this book to help you. So when your puppy is afraid, your first instinct may be to coddle him, stroke him lovingly and whisper soothing sounds into his velvet ears. Unfortunately, this can make your puppy's shyness worse. When you pet your puppy, you are praising the action he is performing at the time you are petting him. If he's cowering, shivering, or whining, you are praising that behavior. Oops! You want your puppy to be confident. Make sure you only praise him when he is acting that way. Otherwise, your puppy may think there is really something to be afraid of, since you're all worked up about it, too. Your puppy is very in tune to your feelings, so if you are stressed and upset, he will be, too. The best thing you can do for your puppy is act confident and casual. Let him see you unafraid, and it will go a long way toward teaching him that he has no reason to be afraid himself.

What can you do to help your puppy find his confidence? Take your puppy to a training class. Make sure it is a reward-based class that does not use harsh tools or methods, because those will only make him more fearful. Training classes should not be boot camps; they should be fun places for both people and puppies to learn. Training your puppy will give him confidence as he learns he can get rewarded for accomplishing things. He will also learn that even though he is around strange people and dogs, it's a fun, safe experience.

Your trainer will teach you exercises you can do to help your puppy build his confidence. Here's just one example of how to turn a scary experience into a pleasant one for your puppy:

Step 1: Preparation

1. Make a list of all the things that scare your puppy; the vacuum cleaner, strange people, men, children, etc. Put the list in order. Maybe your puppy is much more afraid of men with beards than the vacuum cleaner. Put the scariest item at the top of your list.

2. Make a list of things your puppy really, really loves; playing ball, cooked hamburger, garlic chicken, cheese, hot dogs, etc. Put the list in order. Maybe your puppy goes more crazy over hot dogs than playing ball. Put the most loved item at the top of your list.

3. With your lists, now you can match up really scary items with really tempting goodies. You now have a good idea of which reward will help balance which fear. For example, if your dog thinks belly rubs are only okay, those may not be enough to deal with his greatest fear.

Step 2: Training

1. It's important when doing this type of exercise to avoid the common

mistakes we've listed. You cannot push your dog past his point of success, or you will make him more afraid. You'll note this is a gradual process, and that's normal. If your puppy is afraid of something, he won't be cured overnight. Taking your time in the short run will help you on the long run.

2. We'll use the example of a puppy who freaks out when you try and clip his nails, but loves peanut butter.

3. Get your nail clippers and a large spoon holding a big glob of peanut butter.

Turn scary experiences into pleasant ones for your puppy by conditioning your puppy slowly and using rewards and praise.

4. Show your dog the clippers and immediately give him the peanut butter. You can gently scrape the spoon on the roof of his mouth so he starts licking the peanut butter.

5. While he's licking, just show him the clippers. Then put the spoon and clippers away.

6. Repeat several times throughout the day. Make sure the peanut butter and clippers always appear and disappear together. When your puppy starts getting excited at the sight of them, you're ready for the next step.

Practical Solutions to Pesky Problems

Step 3: Reinforcement

1. Give your puppy the peanut butter as usual, but this time, quickly touch the clippers to his paw. Just touch and go; don't hold them there. Praise when you touch his paw.

2. Repeat until your puppy doesn't mind you touching his nails with the clippers. This may take several tries over several days, or it might happen very quickly; either way is fine.

3. Give your puppy the peanut butter, then gently pick up his foot and quickly touch the clippers to a nail; just touch quickly and let go. Praise your puppy if he doesn't squirm.

4. Work up to where you can touch the clipper to all paws, but only proceed if your puppy does not get fidgety. When your puppy is fine

If your puppy is exposed to other pets on a regular basis, he will get along with almost anyone.

The most important thing you can do for your puppy is to teach him how to adjust to life in his new home and how to get along with your family.

with you touching the clipper to all paws, it's time to move on to the next step.

Step 4: Advanced Training

1. Give your puppy the peanut butter, then clip *one* nail. Success! Praise your puppy, praise yourself, and quit for the day. There is no law written anywhere that says you have to clip a puppy's toenails all in one sitting.

2. The next day, clip another nail. Repeat this, day by day, until your puppy doesn't mind you clipping nails at all. Your patience will pay off, and your puppy will be much easier to handle.

This exercise paired up a scary thing, cutting nails, with a good thing, yummy peanut butter. By pairing them up over time, your puppy begins

Your puppy should give up his toys or let you near his food bowl without growling or snapping.

to associate the good thing with the scary thing so that it's not so scary after all. A professional dog trainer can help you use this concept with other things that frighten your puppy so that he learns the world has much more good things in it than scary ones.

The Aggressive Puppy: Growling, Snapping, Biting

You've learned to stay away from your puppy's food bowl because every time you go near it, he growls at you. He must really love his rawhide chews, because he won't let anyone near him when he has those. He's decided he likes lying on the bed and the couch, too; just don't try and move him or he'll snap. Maybe you have a puppy who's an angel with people but turns into a raging devil with other dogs. You're wondering if this will just go away as he gets older or whether it will get worse and he'll bite. Maybe he already has bitten, but it really wasn't his fault—was it?

Your Outta Control Puppy

Some growls are hard to interpret if you're not used to the vocalizations that puppies make. If your puppy growls when he plays with his toys, that doesn't mean he's ready to start a canine crime spree—he's like a kid making sound effects when he plays with his soldiers. But if your puppy growls at you when you pick him up, try to get near his things, or try to take away something from him, if he has snapped at you or bitten you, then you have an aggression problem. And this is a very serious problem indeed.

It may crush you to think that your dog is aggressive. Why is he lashing out at you? Haven't you given him everything? A wonderful home, lots of toys, and affection, but those things are not in question here. There are many reasons why a puppy could be aggressive.

* Aggressive parents. Temperament is passed down from parent to puppy.

* Poor socialization. If your puppy has not been introduced to lots of humans, then he can't possibly understand how humans behave, and it may be frightening to him. Dogs that are frightened often lash out, figuring that the best defense is a good offense.

Proper socialization is an important part of good behavior. If your dog acts aggressively, he has probably had success with this behavior in the past and has learned that it gets him what he wants.

* Harsh methods. Aggression begets aggression, so if someone has spanked, scruff shaked, or used a rolled-up

newspaper or other such method to discipline your puppy, then your puppy may have learned that's the way to deal with situations. "This person spanked me, so I guess I'm supposed to spank back." A puppy can't roll up a newspaper, so he'll use his teeth.

* Past success. He's learned that being pushy works. Your puppy paws you over and over again to throw his ball, and you do it, just to get him to leave you in peace for a few seconds. He's just learned that he can get what he wants by pawing you. If he cries, you feed him. If he slams you with his wet nose in the middle of the night, you let him outside. One day, he growls at you when you reach for his toy, and you immediately back off. He's learned growling is really successful. You now, basically, have a brat on your hands.

Harsh discipline or teasing can cause puppies to act aggressively. Make sure you always treat your puppy with the utmost respect and kindness.

Your Outta Control Puppy

Some aggressive behavior can be passed on from parents to puppy. It is best to consult a professional trainer when dealing with any aggression problems.

Now, we are *not* saying you should push back. If your puppy growls over his toys, and you decide to stand up to him one day and take that toy, you could get bitten in the process. Remember, just because you can take possession of the toy doesn't mean another family member can. There are other ways to work with your puppy that are safer and more successful.

Dealing with an aggressive puppy presents serious challenges. If you have children in your life, they are especially vulnerable to dog bites. Children often don't recognize the puppy's signals to get them to go away, such as lifting his lip, growling, etc., so the puppy tries harder and harder to tell the child to leave and eventually bites to get his point across. Also, dogs don't award children the same status they do adults. If your puppy were to bite someone or hurt another dog, you would feel awful, and you could be in big trouble. In today's society, a dog bite is a speed ticket to court. Are you ready to lose your house in a lawsuit?

Practical Solutions to Pesky Problems

Aggression will not just go away on its own. You need professional guidance.

We can't possibly cover all you need to understand about living with an aggressive puppy here in this book, but we can offer you some first-aid tips to use until you get professional help in person. First, avoid these common mistakes.

✳ Pretending there isn't really a problem. Let's face it; no one wants to admit they have an aggressive dog. Many owners come up with creative excuses to avoid the painful truth, sometimes even taking the blame themselves for their battle scars: "Oh, it was completely my fault. I shouldn't have picked him up so quickly. I must have frightened him and that's why he bit me." "He was a stray and I guess it's hard for him to realize no one is going to hurt him, so that's why he bit me when I reached for his bone." "I think he was dozing on the couch and I must have startled him, so he bit me."

Until your dog is trustworthy, take away his opportunities to act aggressively and use good management techniques until you can teach him healthier alternatives.

Excuses will not help you and they will not help your puppy. They will just hide the problem, which will grow worse and worse. It's very hard to admit your puppy is aggressive, but know this—an aggressive puppy

Your Outta Control Puppy

is not an evil puppy. Your puppy is probably affectionate, sweet, smart, and you love him very much, which you should. He's a member of your family. Your puppy just has some triggers that are not very nice and could end up being dangerous. You have to admit they exist so you can get help.

* Punishing your puppy when he growls. Growling is communication—your puppy is trying to tell you something. If you yell at him or spank him every time he growls, you may accidentally be treating the symptom, not the problem. For example, let's say your puppy has never really been around a lot of other dogs. One day you take him for a walk and another dog approaches. Your puppy growls and lunges at the other dog, because it's an alien to him. He's never seen another creature like that before, and he's afraid. You yell at your puppy and yank his collar. Did that teach your puppy not to be afraid? Nope. Instead, you may have taught your puppy that he really should be afraid of that other dog, because the sight of that dog made you upset and caused him pain.

So now his fear grows worse, except you taught him not to tell you about it. One day another dog comes right up to your puppy, and your puppy "suddenly" bites the other dog. Your punishment didn't treat the cause—your puppy's fear—it just treated the symptom—your puppy's growling. An aggressive puppy is like a teapot; the stressful steam has to go somewhere. If you block one outlet, it will just find another to break through.

So now you're ready to face this problem ... but how do you start? Here are some tips to get you started.

* Get professional help. Find a professional pet dog trainer or applied animal behaviorist to help you tackle this serious issue, either with private lessons or a specially designed course,

sometimes called "growl classes," just for aggressive dogs. Get recommendations from your veterinarian and friends, and if you see a nicely behaved dog with its owner in the neighborhood, ask who helped train him. You can also visit the Association of Pet Dog Trainers (APDT) web site at www.apdt.com and search for trainers from its directory.

✳ Interview the trainer carefully. Ask if you can sit in and observe a class (without your puppy, of course). See if the students and dogs are having fun and learning, and if the trainer is a good communicator and an excellent coach. Ask if the trainer has experience working with aggression cases and what types of methods she uses. You're looking for someone who has a great understanding of learning theory and uses reward-based methods, not someone who promises to "teach your puppy who's the boss." Also, make sure that *you* will be an integral part of the training process. Instead of sending your puppy away to work with a stranger, you need to learn how to deal with your puppy's issues and improve how you interact with your puppy. Make sure the trainer is going to train you.

✳ Manage your puppy's triggers until you can learn how to better deal with them. For example, does your puppy growl on the bed when you try to get her off? Then don't let her on the bed anymore. This isn't being mean, it's being smart. She thinks the bed is hers—it's not. It's your bed—you paid for it. If she can't be nice on the bed, then she hasn't earned the right to be on the bed. After you work with a professional to improve her behavior, then she may earn the privilege again later.

✳ Does your puppy only growl over her chewable bones? No more bones then. If your puppy can't play nice with toys, then she

If your dog is possessive of a particular toy, don't let her play with
it until she can learn acceptable behavior.

doesn't get to play with them at all until she learns more
acceptable behavior.

* If your puppy is aggressive with strangers, be very, very careful
  with his interactions with people. You don't want to risk a bite. For
  example, don't take him to the middle of a crowded park. Some
  folks think that's a good way to socialize their puppies and get
  them used to people, but for an aggressive puppy, it's too much all
  at once.

Remember, every time your puppy growls, snaps, or bites, that's giving
him a chance to practice that behavior. Take away his practice
opportunities and use good management until you can teach him
healthier alternatives.

Friends for Life

O wning an outta control puppy can make you feel like you will never have a dog you can live with in peace. Sometimes puppies miss out on fun because they're just too unmanageable to take anywhere. A neglected puppy is one that develops bad habits and behavioral problems, so it ends up being a sad circle.

By now, you don't have to settle for an outta control situation, and you have some first-aid tools to help you get on track. Stock up on your patience, be consistent, and teach your puppy what you want him to do, and that perfect angel puppy you brought home the first day

If you deal with all your puppy's behavior problems at this stage in his life, you will have a wonderful companion and friend.

will be back and better than ever.

Puppyhood is just a blip on the radar of a dog's life. Your puppy will outgrow some of his antics as he reaches maturity, but some problems will get worse if not addressed. If you tackle your problems now, you will have a wonderful adult dog companion.

It will be hard work. Training a puppy takes determination and real effort, but the results are worth it. Just think, soon you can have a puppy that doesn't embarrass you in front of your friends. Your family members will welcome you and your pup into their homes instead of making excuses why he can't visit, and you'll be able to take your puppy all sorts of places that you didn't dare before. There is a variety of fun activities you can share with your previously outta control puppy.

Agility

Agility is a competition sport in which dogs run through an obstacle course. The goal is to get through the course with the best time and without any mistakes. There are tunnels, tires to leap through, jumps to go over, A-frames and dogwalks to run over, teeter totters to navigate, and more. Please note that puppies must be fully grown to safely do the jumps.

Your Outta Control Puppy

Dogs compete in size categories, so Corgis don't have to go head-to-head with Border Collies.

This sport is great for very active, agile dogs. If you have an outta control puppy who leaps over your coffee table, this may be his true calling. First, you have to teach your dog basic exercises, such as sit, down, and especially coming when called. Beginning agility is taught on leash, but eventually you go off leash, so you need a dog that won't leave the course and run amok through the neighborhood.

Agility can build confidence in shy dogs. It's also great exercise for your dog and you. Local dog trainers, agility or obedience clubs offer classes, and there are several national organizations that sponsor agility trials, some of which only allow purebreds to compete and some that take all dogs. You can compete for ribbons and titles or just train for the fun and exercise.

Obedience

Take training your puppy to the next level by competing in obedience trials. You can earn ribbons and titles for your dog. It can get pretty competitive, so make sure you and your puppy are in it for fun, not ego.

Dogs must perform specific exercises in a ring, and the

Training your puppy for obedience or dog sports will make your relationship stronger.

Once you control problem behavior and start basic obedience, you and your dog can start the real fun!

exercises get harder with each level you try to attain. Beginning titles feature leash work, recalls, and basic commands, while higher titles require your dog to choose and retrieve an article that smells like you from several dropped on the ground. Your dog will also need to sit and down for a set number of minutes with a group of other dogs. When competing for the higher titles, you'll even have to leave the room while your dog stays put.

You start with a set number of points, and a judge tells you when to perform each exercise. Any mistakes are subtracted from your total score.

Local dog trainers and obedience clubs offer classes, and there are several national organizations that sponsor obedience trials, some which allow only purebreds to compete and some that take all dogs, even ones with disabilities.

Rally-O

A new dog sport that is gaining in popularity is Rally Obedience, or Rally-O competition. Rally-O is fun, fast-paced, and not as formal as traditional obedience competition. For pet owners who don't enjoy the competitive atmosphere of traditional obedience, Rally-O is an exciting option.

There are signs set up on a course, each with a different exercise. You follow the course with your dog, and when you reach a sign, you complete the exercise on that sign. You start with a set number of points. A judge follows along behind you and takes off points for any mistakes. Also, unlike traditional obedience competition, you can encourage your dog throughout the course. You can earn ribbons and titles in Rally-O. The courses get harder with each level you pursue.

The AKC offers Rally-O competition for purebred dogs, and the APDT offers Rally-O competition for all dogs. With APDT Rally-O, you have the option to use food as a reward during the course, and it offers categories for children to participate as well.

Flyball

Does your puppy live to fetch balls? Then flyball may be the perfect outlet for him. A team sport, flyball is a relay race. Each team features four dogs, who each run a straight line over four hurdles to a box with a spring-loaded lever. When the dogs push the lever, the box spits out a tennis ball. The dogs must then run back over the hurdles to the start line.

Most retrievers excel at any sport that requires them to fetch something.

Friends for Life

Dogs need basic training to keep them under control, and they must get along well with other dogs. This fast-paced sport is exciting to watch, and, since you need a team, you can make some great dog friends, too.

Canine Freestyle

Does your puppy have style? Do you enjoy dancing? This hot sport combines training with fancy footwork. With Canine Freestyle, you take basic and advanced obedience moves and choreograph them to music.

Dogs heel forward and backward, do figure eights around their handler's legs, wave, bow and more, but, most of all, they have a blast. If your idea of the perfect dance partner is your dog, then this might be for you. Canine Freestyle is more popular in some parts of the country than others, so it may be difficult to find a class in your area, but you can order videotapes and books explaining the sport if a local class is not available.

With proper training, any sweet-tempered, well-mannered puppy can grow up to be an excellent therapy dog.

Therapy Volunteers

Does your puppy experience stranger-love-at-first-sight? Is he confident in different environments? Visiting patients in health care facilities with your dog can be heartwarming and rewarding. There are several national organizations

Building a strong foundation between you and your puppy will create a lifelong bond between you.

that screen and register dogs. It's important to go through a program because it makes sure your dog is suited for the work and it provides you with liability insurance. Many people think that just because Fluffy is friendly, she can visit nursing homes. But if Fluffy accidentally scratches a patient when jumping off a lap or gets tangled in an IV, you could have a lawsuit on your hands, and most facility volunteer insurance policies do not cover dog-related incidents.

Overall, puppies must be at least one year to participate and have impeccable manners. They must love being handled by strangers all over their bodies and cannot react to loud noises or the sight of health care equipment. If you have the time to volunteer, animal-assisted therapy is such a wonderful activity to share with your best friend, and you will be making many people smile with your visits.

Tracking

Does your puppy love to follow his nose? You may have a tracking star on your hands. You can compete for ribbons and titles in tracking, or just train for the fun of it. If your puppy has the aptitude, you can even train him to find people. Ask your local dog-training club if it offers tracking classes. If not, the folks there may be able to point you to someone who does in your area.

If your puppy loves to follow his nose, you may have a future tracking champion on your hands.

Canine Good Citizen

The AKC offers a Canine Good Citizen (CGC) test for dogs to show they are well-mannered family companions. This is not a competition. There are ten exercises, and your dog must pass all ten in order to pass the test. All dogs can participate, even mixed-breed dogs, as long as they are old enough to have had their rabies vaccination. If your dog passes, you'll get a certificate honoring his good manners.

Sharing Your Life

Whether you choose to pursue a formal sport or activity or just enjoy hanging out with your puppy, he's a member of your family. The more you include him in your everyday activities, the more he will bond with you and want to work for you. The more time you spend training him, the more he'll learn what you want. Keep it up, and you could end up being a role model for other puppy owners.

Just imagine—you could be walking with your puppy one day and someone will stop you and exclaim, "Your puppy is so much better behaved than mine!"

Wouldn't that be something? You can do it—you don't have to settle for outta control, because underneath that monster behavior lies a wonderful canine companion. You can work with your puppy to bring out his best, and you'll forge a lasting relationship along the way.

Resources

Books

Adamson, Eve. *The Simple Guide to a Healthy Dog*.
(New Jersey: TFH, 2002.)

Aloff, Brenda. *Positive Reinforcement: Training Dogs in the Real World*.
(New Jersey: TFH, 2001.)

Bonham, Margaret. *The Simple Guide to Getting Active with Your Dog*.
(New Jersey: TFH, 2001.)

Donaldson, Jean. *The Culture Clash*.
(California: James & Kenneth Publishers, 1996.)

Dunbar, Dr. Ian. *After You Get Your Puppy*.
(California: James & Kenneth Publishers, 2001.)

Dunbar, Dr. Ian. *Dog Behavior*.
(New York: Howell Book House, 1999.)

Dunbar, Dr. Ian. *How to Teach a New Dog Old Tricks*.
(California: James & Kenneth Publishers, 1996.)

Jones, Dr. Deborah. *Clicker Fun*.
(Maine: Howln Moon Press, 1998.)

London, Dr. Karen & McConnell, Dr. Patricia. *Feeling Outnumbered? How to Manage and Enjoy Your Multi-Dog Household*.
(Wisconsin: Dog's Best Friend, Ltd., 2001.)

McConnell, Dr. Patricia. *How to Be the Leader of the Pack ... and Have Your Dog Love You For It!*
(Wisconsin: Dog's Best Friend, Ltd. 2002.)

Miller, Pat. *The Power of Positive Dog Training*.
(New York: Hungry Minds, Inc., 2001.)

Pryor, Karen. *Don't Shoot the Dog! The New Art of Teaching and Training.*
(New York: Bantam, 1999.)

Rugaas, Turid. *On Talking Terms with Dogs: Calming Signals.*
(Hawaii: Legacy By Mail, 1997.)

Organizations

American Kennel Club (AKC)
5580 Centerview Drive, Suite 250
Raleigh, NC 27606-3389
Phone: 919-233-9796
www.akc.org

American Mixed Breed Obedience Registration (AMBOR)
179 Niblick Road #113
Paso Robles, CA 93446
Phone: 805-226-9275
E-mail: ambor@amborusa.org
www.amborusa.org

Association of Pet Dog Trainers (APDT)
Note: You can visit the APDT website and find a member trainer in your
area.
5096 Sand Road SE
Iowa City, IA 52240-8217
Phone: 1-800-PET-DOGS
www.apdt.com
Note: APDT Rally-O is open to purebreds and mixed-breed dogs.
P.O. Box 5817
Chattanooga, TN 37406

Certification Council for Pet Dog Trainers (CCPDT)
Note: The CCPDT serves to establish and maintain a series of standards for professional competence by offering the first national certification for the dog training industry. Certified trainers can use the Certified Pet Dog Trainer (CPDT) designation, and must earn continuing education credits to keep the title.
E-mail: merctt@aol.com
www.ccpdt.org

Delta Society

Note: This program also accepts all domestic animals who can pass the screening, including cats, rabbits, guinea pigs, and more.

875 124th Ave. NE, Ste 101
Bellevue, WA 98005
Phone: 425-226-7357
Fax: 425-235-1076
E-mail: info@deltasociety.org
www.deltasociety.org

North American Dog Agility Council (NADAC)

Note: NADAC trials are open to purebred and mixed-breed dogs.

11522 South Hwy 3
Cataldo, ID 83810
Phone: 208-689-3803
E-mail: info@nadac.com
www.nadac.com

North American Flyball Association

P.O. Box 512
1400 West Devon Ave.
Chicago, IL 60660
Phone: 1-800-318-6312
E-mail: flyball@flyball.org
www.flyball.org

North Shore Animal League

25 Davis Avenue
Port Washington, NY 11050
Phone: 516-883-7575
E-mail: nsal1@aol.com
www.nsalamerica.org

Therapy Dogs Incorporated

P.O. Box 5868
Cheyenne, WY 82003
Phone: 877-843-7364
E-mail: therdog@sisna.com
www.therapydogs.com

Therapy Dogs International, Inc.
88 Bartley Road
Flanders, NJ 07836
Phone: 973-252-9800
E-mail: tdi@gti.net
www.tdi-dog.org

United Kennel Club (UKC)
Note: UKC trials are open to UKC permanently registered, limited privilege, or temporarily registered dogs.
100 East Kilgore Road
Kalamazoo, Michigan 49002-5584
Phone: 269-343-9020
Fax: 269-343-7037
www.ukcdogs.com

United States Dog Agility Association (USDAA)
Note: USDAA trials are open to purebred and mixed-breed dogs.
P.O. Box 850995
Richardson, Texas 75085-0955
Phone: 972-487-2200
Fax: 972-272-4404
E-mail: info@usdaa.com
www.usdaa.com

World Canine Freestyle Organization (WCFO)
P.O. Box 350122
Brooklyn, NY 11235-2525
E-mail: wcfodogs@aol.com
www.worldcaninefreestyle.org

Index

Photos:

Teoti Anderson: p. 117
Paulette Braun: p. 26, P. 115
Tara Darling: p. 23
Judith Strom: p. 22
Karen Taylor: p. 74
All other photos by Isabelle Francais